EXTEND

WORD Processing

Exam success at Stage II

Carol McKenzie

Pat Bryden

Heinemann Educational,
a division of Heinemann Publishers (Oxford) Ltd,
Halley Court, Jordan Hill, Oxford OX2 8EJ

OXFORD LONDON EDINBURGH MADRID ATHENS BOLOGNA
PARIS MELBOURNE SYDNEY AUCKLAND SINGAPORE TOKYO
IBADAN NAIROBI HARARE GABORONE PORTSMOUTH NH (USA)

First Published 1994

95 96 97 11 10 9 8 7 6 5 4 3 2

A catalogue record for this book is available from the British Library on request.

ISBN 0 435 453017

Designed by Ken Vail Graphic Design, Cambridge using Quark XPress 3.1™
on the Apple Macintosh™ Ci

Printed in Great Britain by Thomson Litho, East Kilbride, Scotland

Acknowledgements
The authors and publishers would like to thank the RSA for permission to
reproduce examination requirements and the list of standard abbreviations.

Contents

Contents

Extending Word Processing has been written as a continuation text to *Introducing Word Processing** by the same authors. It has been designed as a progressive course and is suitable for use in the classroom, in an open-learning workshop or as a private study aid.

Extending Word Processing will help those preparing to take an intermediate examination in word processing, using any suitable software package. However, the book would be equally useful to those who simply wish to extend their working knowledge of word processing.

Coverage

This book is designed for those of you preparing to take the RSA Stage II Word Processing examination. Units 1 to 5 cover Part 1 of the Stage II examination. Units 6 to 10 cover Part 2 of the Stage II examination.

Assessment

At the end of Unit 5 you should be able to do an RSA Stage II Part 1 paper:

    a   within a *one-and-a-quarter-hour* time limit
    b   with no more than eight accuracy and five presentation errors for a *Pass*
    c   with no more than three accuracy and three presentation errors for a *Distinction*.

At the end of Unit 10 you should be able to do an RSA Stage II Part 2 paper:

    a   within a *one-and-a-quarter-hour* time limit
    b   with no more than four accuracy and three presentation errors for a *Pass*
    c   with no more than two accuracy and two presentation errors for a *Distinction*.

Previous experience

It is assumed that you have completed an elementary (Stage I) word processing course and are therefore familiar with conventional document layout and basic text-processing principles and practice. You should also be familiar with the hardware you are going to use (including the printer).

* This publication covers the following syllabuses:
    RSA Computer Literacy and Information Technology
    (word processing application)
    RSA Core Text Processing Skills (taken on a word processor)
    RSA Stage I Word Processing

Format

Units 1 to 3 and **6 to 8** take you through the word processing functions you need to know for RSA Stage II examinations. Instructions for the preparation of particular documents are given at the beginning of each unit, followed by practice exercises.

Consolidation practice for each part of Stage II is available in Units 4 and 9, i.e., after all the topics for each part of each syllabus have been covered.

Mock examinations for each part of Stage II are provided in Units 5 and 10.

Print-out checks for all exercises are included in the book and these may be used for checking by both students and teachers/trainers.

The progress review checklist can be used to record progress throughout the book – in learning and in accuracy.

Command boxes for all word processing functions are inserted to show that you need to learn the commands relevant to your software in order to carry out a new word processing function. (At some points, command boxes relating to previously learnt functions have been included as revision.) These command boxes are intended as points of reference to draw your attention to the need to consult the glossary of commands in the centre of the book.

The glossary of commands gives space alongside each function for the insertion of the appropriate software commands. Once the (pull-out) glossary is fully completed, you will be able to use it as a quick reference to functions and commands:

- If you are working on you own, refer to the software manufacturer's manual and insert the command sequence in the space provided against the command boxes in the glossary.

- If you are using the book as a tutor for a group of students, you could take a photocopy of the blank glossary and then insert the command sequences in the spaces provided against the command boxes. You could then photocopy the completed glossary for distribution to your students.

How to use this book

If you are preparing for an examination, you are advised to work through the book unit by unit.

The book has been planned as a progressive course and some of the work you will do in the later units is based on text you keyed in earlier so it is important to save your work.

Symbols

When you see this symbol, read all the information before you begin.

When you see this symbol, carry out the exercises.

Proofread and spellcheck carefully. Preview your document before saving. Print your work and check against the print-out checks at the back of the book.

At the end of Unit 1 you will have learnt how to:

a   identify errors in a printed document by comparing it against a manuscript original
b   key in a corrected version of the document
c   print a document from your file directory
d   change the line length for a whole document.

Typescript containing typographical errors

Text processing may involve putting right any mistakes made in previous print-outs. Watch out for uncorrected spelling errors and transposition errors.

Examples:

This sentance contains 3 <u>speling errers</u>.

should be keyed in as:

This **sentence** contains 3 **<u>spelling errors</u>**.

This sentence contians 2 <u>transpositoin errors</u>.

should be keyed in as:

This sentence **contains** 2 **<u>transposition</u>** errors.

It is up to you to notice typographical errors, to decide what is wrong and to key in the word correctly.

Proofreading

It is easy to think that, because you have used the spellcheck facility on your word processing system, your work is accurate. Automatic spellchecking is very useful and you should always use spellcheck if it is available on your system, before you save or print a document but you must *also* proofread the document yourself.

The program's spellcheck facility simply compares each word you have keyed in with its own 'dictionary' of words.

Candidates who fail examinations often do so because their proofreading is not adequate. One of the most common errors is the omission of words. Unfortunately, if you have missed out some words, or not deleted some words as instructed, spellchecking will not detect this.

If you have typed the wrong 'version' of a word, e.g. **there** instead of **their**, spellchecking will not detect this as both versions are spelt correctly.

Only *you* can tell if you have copied names of people or places correctly and if a piece of information which you were asked to find is accurate. For example, spellcheck cannot tell if the date you have keyed in for 'Thursday of next week' is the correct one. Don't guess – use a diary or calendar.

The skills of proofreading are essential in text processing. You should train yourself to check every detail in any work you have done *before* you print it so as not to waste paper. It is not enough to check the work on you screen, you must *compare* it with the 'copy' from which you are working – going through it word by word.

SWITCH ON AND LOAD
WP PROGRAM

LOGGED DRIVE (to change)

SPELLCHECK

Follow the instructions step by step.

1.1   Switch on and load your word processing program.

1.2   Insert your work disk in the disk drive and check that your system is set up to save your work to the appropriate drive (usually drive A).

Exercise 1A

1.3   Proofread the following text as instructed. There are 12 errors.

When you have identified all the errors, key in a correct copy and check against the original manuscript. Make any necessary amendments.

Our new junior has made lots of errors!

Please key in a correct copy from the typescript below. Use the manuscript to check that your work is better. Retain justified right margin.

CALDERGHYLL (REF CMB422) ← bold

This mid-terraced house is near the centre of hte town and covenient for allamenities. Luxuriously furnished with antiques and equipped with every every labour-saving device, this house offers the the ideal place for a relaxing break. Acommodation is for 4 people in 2 twin-bedded rooms on the first floor. The ground floor comprises lounge, kitchen and dinning room. The first flor bathroom has both bath and shower.

The owner does not object to one samll dog kept under proper controle. PRICE BAND 12.

NB Available from (1st Sat of next month)

CALDERGHYLL (REF CM424)

This mid-terraced house is near the centre of the town and convenient for all amenities. Luxuriously furnished with antiques and equipped with every labour-saving device, this house offers the ideal place for a relaxing break. Accommodation is for 4 people in 2 twin-bedded rooms on the first floor. The ground floor comprises lounge, kitchen and dining room. The first floor bathroom has both bath and shower. The owner does not object to one small dog kept under proper control. PRICE BAND 12. NB Available from ____.

Printing from the directory of files

When you are preparing for an examination, you should get into the habit of printing from the list files (directory) screen and not from the document itself. (In some programs, this is the only way that printing can be done.)

PRINT OUT HARD COPY

SAVE WORK TO DISK

1 Save your work using the filename given.
2 Call up the directory or list of files (if not already on screen).
3 Move the cursor to highlight the file you wish to print.
4 Follow your program commands to print the file.

1.4 Save and **print** a copy of your work. Use the filename **EX1A**.

Check your work against the print-out at the back of the book.

Changing the line length

You may be asked to change the 'line length' of a document to a fixed number of characters. This is achieved by either *indenting* or *insetting* the margins. (It is not always possible in word processing to be completely accurate in this respect and examiners should be aware of this and lenient in their marking of this feature.)

The width of A4 paper is approximately 8.2 inches (or 82 characters in 10-pitch). Find out the 'default ' margins in your program and the number of characters across a normal typing line.

The extra characters to be added to the margins to reduce the typing line can be incorporated in any of the following three ways:

a   all the required extra characters added to the left margin, *or*

b   all the required extra characters added to the right margin, *or*

c   some of the extra characters added to the right margin and some to the left margin (these amounts do not have to be equal).

Examples:

To change the line length to 50 characters from 62 characters, you would need to increase the margins by 12 characters. You could *change the margin settings* as follows:

- increase the left margin by 12 characters, *or*
- increase the right margin by 12 characters, *or*
- increase both left and right margins by 6 characters each.

To change the line length to 52 characters from 62 characters, you would need to increase the margins by 10 characters. You could change the margins as described above or (if available on your program) you could *use the indent facility* as follows:

- indent the text by 5 spaces *at each side*, *or*
- indent the text by 10 spaces *at the left*.

MARGINS (TO CHANGE)

INDENT FUNCTION

The above examples assume that the indent facility uses default tab settings every 5 character spaces. Check the settings on your program.

Exercise 1B

1.5   Proofread the following text as instructed. When you have identified all the errors, start a new document and key in a correct copy and check against the original manuscript. **Change the line length to 50 characters**.

Make any necessary amendments.

Save and **print** a copy of your work. Use the filename **EX1B**.

Check your work against the print-out check at the back of the book.

My daughter kindly offered to do this on her computer at home. As you can see, it is not perfect! Please produce a correct copy, using a justified right margin.

tHere is no reason why youshould not by overdue products becuase the shopkeeper is obliged to provide goods which meet a certain quality – they must not be "bad or "off". Even if you buy such goods at a reduced price, your legal rights is not affected. If you are unable to obtain staisfaction from the shop manager, contact the local Trading Standards Officer thro' the town Hall.

Most food producers need to maintin a good reputation and and they will usually take any compliant very seriously indeed. It is often a good idea to write to Managing Director of an organisatoin enclosing, if poss, a sample of the defective goods. You may have your costes refunded and sometimes a free gift or sample is sent to you as a token of goodwill.

T S Orwen   (1st Friday of next month) ⟩—bold

There is no reason why you should not buy overdue products because the shopkeeper is obliged to provide goods which meet a certain quality – they must not be "bad" or "off". Even if you buy such goods at a reduced price, your legal rights are not affected. If you are unable to obtain satisfaction from the shop manager, contact the local Trading Standards Officer through the Town Hall.

Most food producers need to maintain a good reputation and they will usually take any complaint very seriously indeed. It is often a good idea to write to the Managing Director of an organisation enclosing, if possible, a sample of the defective goods. You may have your costs refunded and sometimes a free gift or sample is sent to you as a token of goodwill.

T S Orwen (1st Friday of next month)

embolden please

At the end of Unit 2, you will have learnt how to:

a   identify inconsistencies of presentation in text
b   key in text with consistency of presentation
c   insert headers and footers on a document
d   insert page numbering on a letter
e   insert page breaks (pagination) in a two-page letter
f   expand recognized RSA Stage II abbreviations
g   understand text correction signs and make corresponding amendments to text
h   key in a business letter, including special marks and indication of enclosure(s).

Typescript containing correction signs – reminders

A word processor operator is seldom given work which simply requires to be copied exactly as it is. A photocopier could do the job much more quickly! Usually, the 'copy' (text which the operator copies from) contains amendments. Examples:

amended
This sentence has been ~~changed~~.

should be keyed in as **This sentence has been amended**.

Please delete ~~or omit~~ this word.

should be keyed in as **Please delete this word**.

this sentence
Extra words should be inserted for ⁄to make sense.

should be keyed in as **Extra words should be inserted for this sentence to make sense**.

You may be asked to move words or ⟨sentences or⟩ phrases.

should be keyed in as **You may be asked to move sentences or words or phrases**.

Additional text correction signs – reminders

Look at the following examples of other signs which you may see on typewritten or manuscript text.

// or ⌐

Start a new paragraph where you see either of these signs. The letters NP (new paragraph) may also appear in the margin.

The 'run on' sign is used when two paragraphs should be joined together.
To join two paragraphs, put the cursor on the first character of the second paragraph and press ⟵ Del twice.

If you see a tick inside a circle in the margin, look for a word (or words) in the text which has a dotted line underneath it. These two signs mean that you should insert the word with the dotted line underneath, even though it may have been crossed out.

⊘ When you type this sentence, ~~delete~~ insert this word.

should be typed as **When you type this sentence, insert this word.**

word1 word2   This sign means that you should type word2 before word1. This is called transposition.

Two words in sentence this are the wrong way round.

should be typed as **Two words in this sentence are the wrong way round.**

You may also have to transpose words vertically, for example if they are in a list.

Dot Matrix	should be typed as	Dot Matrix
Laser		Ink Jet
Ink Jet		Laser
Thermal		Thermal

Business letter layout – reminders

A business letter is written on behalf of an organization and is printed or typed on the organization's own letterhead, which gives all relevant details such as address, telephone and fax numbers, etc.

In the RSA Stage II Part 1 examination, the letter is printed, after the examination, on plain paper. Letterheaded paper is not used at this stage because of the difficulties there may be in feeding single sheets of paper into certain printers.

Block everything at the left-hand margin – do not indent paragraphs or centre items.

Date the letter with today's date.

Use open punctuation – no indentation except in the body of the letter.

Leave at least one clear line space between the different parts of the letter, and between paragraphs.

If the salutation is formal, e.g., 'Dear Sir or Madam' – finish your letter with the complimentary close: 'Yours faithfully'.

If the salutation is informal, e.g., 'Dear Mrs Smith' – finish your letter with the complimentary close: 'Yours sincerely'.

Leave several clear lines for the person sending the letter to write their signature.

Special marks such as: CONFIDENTIAL, PRIVATE, PERSONAL, URGENT, FOR THE ATTENTION OF... etc., should be given some form of emphasis such as bold, underlining or capitalization. If a letter includes a special mark this should also be included on the envelope.

The enclosure mark is usually placed at the end of a letter or memo with one clear line space above and below it.

Consistency of presentation
Measurements, weights, times, money

You should always be consistent in the way in which you present information within a document. The following are examples of points you should watch out for.

Be consistent in the use of an abbreviation to represent a measurement or weight, such as **mm, cm, ft, in, kg, oz, lb**. For example, don't key in **30"** in one place and **24 in** somewhere else in the document. Be consistent – use either **"** or **in** but not a mixture of the two.

You may leave one space before the abbreviation or no spaces but you must be consistent. For example, don't key in **46kg** in one place and **46 kg** somewhere else in the document.

Stick to the 12-hour clock or the 24-hour clock when using times. For example, don't key in **1600 hrs** in one place and **7.30 am** somewhere else in the document. Be consistent in the use of **pm, o'clock, hrs**.

When using an abbreviation for currency (e.g. **$, £, DM, FF**), stick to one method of presentation. For example, don't key in **£15** in one place and **£12.50** somewhere else in the document. Both amounts should show the pence – (**£15.00** and **£12.50**). Don't key in **FF100** in one place and **100 French francs** somewhere else in the document. You should use either **£** or **p** but not both together in one amount – **£0.50p** is wrong.

Words and figures

You should be consistent in the way you present numbers within a document. For example, don't key in **40 miles** in one place and **fifty-five miles** somewhere else in the document. Look through the text first and decide on words or figures. Think about these two examples:

a   **1, 234, 650** is difficult to express in words

b   **1** looks strange as the first word of a sentence.

Other possible inconsistencies

You should be consistent in using the dash (-) or the hyphen (-) between words and symbols. The keyboard symbol is the same, the spacing either side of the symbol is different. For example, don't key in **4 - 6** in one place and **16-21** somewhere else in the document. Also, don't key in **4 to 6** in one place and **16-21** somewhere else in the document. The word **to** can also be used in **3 to 4 weeks' time**, **Tuesday to Thursday**. Don't key in **Friday - Sunday** in one place and **Monday to Wednesday** somewhere else in the document.

You should be consistent in the presentation of **per cent**. For example, don't type % in one place and **per cent** somewhere else in the document.

You should be consistent in keying in words which can be spelt in two different ways. For example, don't type **organise** in one place and **organize** somewhere else in the document.

You should be consistent in the amount of space you leave after punctuation. For example, don't leave **1** space after a full stop in one place and **2** spaces after a full stop somewhere else in the document.

You should standardize the layout of any document which you are producing. For example, don't mix paragraph styles (e.g., keep them all blocked to the left *or* all indented) and make all headings the same style (e.g., all in capitals *or* all in lower case and underlined).

Headers and footers

A *header* is a piece of text in the form of a title, heading or reference which appears at the top of all pages of a multi-page document. A *footer* is the same kind of text appearing at the bottom of all pages.

This word processing function allows you to 'set' the headers and footers by keying in the text once only. The header or footer will then automatically appear on all pages.

Headers and footers can usually be *edited* if the text or layout needs to be changed. (It is not usually necessary to delete the header/footer command when an amendment is needed.)

Note: The header/footer text may not show on the screen when you are working on a document but you can usually check that it is present by using the **preview** function within the print menu if this is available in your program.

Using the header function in the Stage II examination

Each sheet printed for the examination should show your name, centre number and task number. When you are producing multi-page documents in an examination, you can save time by including these details in the header so that they will appear on every page.

HEADERS
FOOTERS

To do this, you could key in your name and other details as the first line of the header, then leave a blank line before keying in the requested header text.

Page numbering

It is often necessary for the pages of a document to be numbered. This word processing function allows you to 'set' the page numbering by giving the commands once only. Consecutive page numbers will then appear automatically on all pages.

PAGE NUMBERING

Note: Page numbers may not show on the screen when you are working on a document but you can check that they are present by using the **preview** function within the print menu if this is available in your program.

Page numbering on letters

PAGE NUMBERING (to suppress)

It is usual to omit the page number on the first page of a letter. Word processing programs usually allow you to set page numbering and then to suppress this facility on any given page (e.g., page 1 if you are keying in a letter).

Pagination in multi-page documents and business letters

Page breaks (new page markers) should be inserted in sensible places within a document so that it is easy to read. A word processor operator is expected to know how to do this.

Find out how many lines of text make up one page on your program. There are 70 lines on an A4 sheet so if your top and bottom margins are set at 1" (6 lines) each, this leaves 58 lines on which you can 'type' (70 - 12 = 58).

Most programs show a 'soft' page break on screen when the maximum number of lines has been used. The printer will start printing on a new page at this point.

A 'hard' page break is inserted by the operator and is usually displayed slightly differently on screen. You should get into the habit of inserting 'hard' page breaks *after* all other text formatting and amendments have been carried out and just before printing.

Consider the following points when paginating (inserting new page markers) in a multi-page document or business letter:

1   The complimentary close of a letter (Yours…, etc.) should never be the *only* text on the last page. Ideally, there should be at least 3 or 4 lines of text above the complimentary close.

2   You should not divide a word between one page and the next.

3   You should not leave only the first line of a paragraph at the bottom of a page (a 'widow').

NEW PAGE MARKER

RETRIEVE FILE

4   You should not carry forward only the last line of a paragraph on to the next page (an 'orphan').

In the following two exercises, you will key in a letter from manuscript copy. The letter will go on to two pages and you will be required to put into practice all the functions and techniques described previously.

You will retrieve the text you keyed in and saved in Unit 1. Read the instructions 2.1 to 2.11 first, then follow them step by step in the order given:

Exercise 2A

2.1   Starting a new document, set a one-line header to show: **Your name Exercise 2A**.

2.2   **Set** page numbering, positioning the number at the foot of the page, and suppressing the page number on page 1.

2.3   **Key in** the letter headed Exercise 2A from manuscript, ensuring that you expand abbreviations and use a consistent style of presentation and layout.

2.4   At the * sign, **retrieve the text** which you saved previously as **EX1A** into the current document.

2.5   **Remove** the justification on the recalled text.

2.6   **Key in** the remainder of the letter.

2.7   **Spellcheck** your letter.

2.8   **Proofread** your letter, comparing it carefully with the manuscript.

2.9   **Paginate** your letter by inserting a new page marker in a suitable place.

2.10 If necessary, **preview** your letter to make sure that the header and page numbering are present.

2.11 **Save** and **print** a copy of your work. Use the filename **EX2A**.

Exercise 2A

Please key in the letter, retrieving text from disk where indicated. Use a ragged right margin throughout and standardise the layout. Save and print your work. Use the file name EX2A.

Ref EWP/2A

Mrs B S Kelly
236 Main Street
Weston
BARNSLEY
BY10 8JJ

Please mark URGENT

Dr Mrs K——

Cumbrian Cottages ← Caps & underline

Thank you for yr letter of (last Monday's date) requesting info on self-catering cottages in Cumbria. I have pleasure in setting out below details of the accom at "Calderghyll" wh is available for ↑wh you mentioned.
the dates

A booking ~~reservation~~ form is enclosed for yr use & I hope that you wl find that you are satisfied w "C——" from the details shown. At this time of yr many people are making holiday arrangements & I wd suggest that you telephone our bookings ~~section~~ dept on 061-763205 as a p in order to make a ↑reservation. ✓
between provisional

You can telephone at any time/8am and 7.00pm from Mon to Fri and between 1000hrs and 5pm from Sat – Sun.

* Retrieve details of Calderghyll saved as EX1A and insert here

I wd like to take this opp of assuring you of the high standards of service from our org. wh you can expect [We pride ourselves on the careful and thorough processing of bookings & enquiries. All of our properties are regularly inspected & members of staff are available at ~~all~~ any time to solve any problems wh may arise.

Please contact me if you wd like any further info or advice.
I look forward to hearing from you in the near future.
insurance
We recom that you take advantage of our inexpensive/cover. The cost is competitive at £4.50 per person per week, and 15 pounds for a family (4-6 persons).

Yrs scly

Elisabeth W Pendragon
RURAL IDYLLS PLC

Abbreviations

There are additional abbreviations for Stages II and III. The abbreviations are not followed by a full stop as they were in Stage I. A complete list is given below:

accom	accommodation	misc	miscellaneous
a/c(s)	account(s)	necy	necessary
ack	acknowledge	opp(s)	opportunity/ies
advert(s)	advertisement	org	organisation
altho'	although	p/t	part time
appt(s)	appointment(s)	poss	possible
approx	approximately	rec(s)	receipt(s)
asap	as soon as possible	rec	receive
bel	believe	recd	received
bus	business	recom	recommend
cat(s)	catalogue(s)	ref(s)	reference(s)
cttee(s)	committee(s)	refd	referred
co(s)	company(ies)	resp	responsible
def	definitely	sec(s)	secretary/ies
dev	develop	sep	separate
dr	dear	sig(s)	signature(s)
ex	exercise	suff	sufficient
exp(s)	expense(s)	temp	temporary
exp	experience	thro'	through
f/t	full time	sh	shall
gov(s)	government(s)	shd	should
gntee(s)	guarantee(s)	wh	which
immed	immediately	wd	would
hrs	hours	w	with
incon	inconvenient/ence	wl	will
info	information	yr(s)	year(s)
mfr(s)	manufacturer(s)	yr(s)	your(s)

Days of the week:

Mon	Monday
Tues	Tuesday
Wed	Wednesday

Words in address

Cres	Crescent
Dr	Drive
Rd	Road

Months of the year:

Jan	January
Feb	February
Mar	March

Complimentary close:

ffly	faithfully
scly	sincerely

Note: You should *retain* other commonly used abbreviations, such as **etc**, **eg**, **NB**, **&** (in company names – *not* **&** in text).

You may *not* take the above list with you into the examination. However, don't forget that you are allowed to use your spellcheck facility and, of course, you may use a dictionary.

Exercise 2B

2.12 Starting a new document, key in the following letter, incorporating the text you produced in **EX1B** at the point shown. Follow the same procedures in the same order as for Exercise 2A by following steps 2.1 to 2.11. **Save** and **print** a copy of your work. Use the filename **EX2B**.

Ref TSO/WP/2B

←———————— FOR THE ATTENTION OF MS W GOOD

The Consumer Guide
172-175 Byre Street
YORK   YO2 1JM

Dr Sirs/~~Madam~~

(LETTERS PAGE) — emphasise

I recently recd a request from yr org for a contribution to yr Consumer Info column, wh I have pleasure in setting out below.

Indent ½" at left only

(Not at its best?) ← caps and bold

* There is no reason.... (EX1B)

It is poss that you are already aware of the fact that it is not unknown for ~~some~~ certain people to take advantage of a mfr's generosity by frequently returning 'faulty' ✓goods ~~products~~. Most mfrs keep records of these transactions so it is not a practice wh I wd recom and it involves more

NP   ~~than~~ (effort and time) than it is worth. [Altho' there is considerable exp in postage, some people have almost made a p/t job out of this ~~pastime~~ hobby!]

Do you think that an extra paragraph to this effect wd be useful ∧for yr readers?
(or relevant)

FOOD ADDITIVES
I hope to hear from you asap on my article on food additives as you said you may be interested in this. ←

Please let me know yr decision both on the text (submitted) and the ~~extra~~ info.
additional

I enclose my bus card so that you may telephone me. I am in f/t employment so you can reach me between the hours of 9.00 am & 1700 hrs at my bus number. After 6 pm I can be contacted at home.

Yrs ffly

T S O___ (Mr)

At the end of Unit 3 you will have learnt how to:

a   insert page breaks within a multi-page document
b   format text to a specified layout
c   work logically through the editing of a document
d   move around the document using 'quick' methods
e   delete text using 'quick' methods
f   search and replace text globally
g   align text to the right
h   use headers, footers and page numbering effectively
i   print documents from the directory.

Page breaks within a multi-page document

Sometimes you are asked to *leave page breaks as shown* or *retain page breaks* in a multi-page document. (Watch out for this instruction in an examination.) Sometimes you are expected to *use your own judgement* as to the most suitable position(s) for new pages to begin.

If you cannot fit all the text you require on a certain page, you could decrease the size of the bottom margin to $1/2$ inch or less if necessary – it is usually defaulted to 1 inch. Look back at the notes in Unit 2 to remind yourself of the 'rules' on pagination.

Multi-page document – formatting requirements

You will be expected to make the following formatting changes in the RSA Stage II Part 1 examination:

Leaving clear line spaces (e.g. for photograph)
Remember there are 6 lines to 1 inch: to leave 1 inch clear you must leave 6 clear lines.

Insetting margins (changing margin settings)
Remember there are 10 characters to 1 inch in 10-pitch.

Indenting text (using indent facility)
Remember to check your default tab settings – usually set at $1/2$ inch. You may have to indent at left only or at both sides.

Moving blocks of text and copying blocks of text
Read the instructions carefully – don't confuse the terms 'move' and 'copy':

Move a block means that the text appears in one place only – you simply have to reposition the block.
Copy a block means that the text appears in two (or more) places – you leave the block in its original position *and* put an identical copy of it in another position.

In an examination, if you 'move' a block instead of 'copy' a block, you will get a lot of accuracy errors as every missing word counts as one error!

Leaving clear line spaces between separate parts of a document
You should leave at least one clear line space in the following situations:

1   between paragraphs and separate parts of a document

2   before and after headings

3   between listed items (such as 1, 2, and 3 as shown here).

COPY BLOCK OF TEXT

MOVE BLOCK OF TEXT

Remember that there is a minimum measurement required for margins. If you add together the left and right margins they should come to at least 1 inch. If you add together the top and bottom margins, they should also come to at least 1 inch.

Organizing text editing in a multi-page document

When a document runs into several pages and there are many changes to be made, you may sometimes feel that you have become 'lost' – particularly if you have been distracted.

The following is a *suggested* method of working which you might like to adopt. Using this method means that you will return to the top of the document and work through it several times carrying out a different function each time. This might seem time consuming but if you always use the method you will get into a routine and you will be sure that you have not missed out anything.

There is an added advantage in going through a document several times – you might spot an error which can be corrected as you scan through the work!

After setting headers and page numbering and viewing to check that they are correct:

1   Carry out all the necessary **text amendments**, e.g., inserting or deleting of text *throughout the whole document.*

2   **Move** blocks of text and **copy** blocks of text as requested *throughout the whole document.*

3   **Search** and **replace** as requested.

4   **Allocate space** (clear line spaces) and **indent** or **inset** margins as requested.

5   **Paginate** your document as requested or as you think fit (read the instructions).

6   **Spellcheck** the whole document.

7   **Proofread** the whole document, comparing word for word with the copy.

8   **Preview** your document (if this facility is available) to make sure that it is going to be printed correctly.

9   And finally, **print** your work.

Moving around the document – advanced methods

When you are checking and proofreading a multi-page document, you need to be able to move the cursor quickly from one section to another. Most programs have quick commands to enable you to do this.

Practise the quick cursor movements so that you become very familiar with them and use them regularly.

CURSOR MOVEMENT –

TO START OF LINE
TO END OF LINE
TO TOP OF SCREEN
TO BOTTOM OF SCREEN
TO TOP OF PREVIOUS PAGE
TO TOP OF NEXT PAGE
TO START OF DOCUMENT
TO END OF DOCUMENT
TO SPECIFIED PAGE
LEFT/RIGHT WORD BY WORD

Deleting text – advanced methods

Most programs have quick commands to enable you to delete blocks of text. Practise the quick text-deletion commands so that you become very familiar with them and use them regularly. Be careful when deleting text! If you find that you have deleted too much text, you can restore it provided you do so immediately.

DELETE –

WORD LEFT/RIGHT OF CURSOR

DELETE FROM –

CURSOR TO END OF LINE
CURSOR TO END OF SENTENCE
CURSOR TO END OF PAGE

RESTORE DELETED TEXT

VIEW DOCUMENT

You are going to work on the text you created and saved as **EX2A** but *before* you retrieve the document, set the format (headers, page numbering, etc.) by following steps 3.1 to 3.4 below.

Exercise 3A

3.1 Starting a new document, set a three-line header as follows:

Name Unit 3 Exercise 3A	(Line 1)
(leave one clear line here)	(Line 2)
RURAL IDYLLS	(Line 3)

Note: Use the header function in this way when practising examination work to ensure that your name, centre number and task number appear on every page printed.

In 'real life', of course, your name would not be required on the document.

3.2 Set page numbering to appear at the *bottom left* of every page.

3.3 Preview your document, if possible, to check that the headers and page numbering are present.

3.4 You may choose whether to use a ragged or a justified right margin – set the format according to your choice.

Multi-page document

3.5 Retrieve your file **EX2A**. Remove any page numbering command or code contained in the retrieved text.

3.6 Delete the reference, date, name and address and salutation from the letter. (Use the quick methods described earlier in this unit.)

3.7 Delete the complimentary close (Yours sincerely … Enc).

3.8 Amend the text in Exercise 3A as shown, inserting hard page-break markers to place the text on three pages as shown. Refer to the glossary to remind yourself about *insetting text* (by changing the margin settings) and *indenting text* (using the indent facility).

(Single line spacing please. Keep page breaks as shown.)

CUMBRIAN COTTAGES — spaced caps, centre, no underline
(underline as heading)

~~Thank you for your letter of (correct date inserted for last Monday) requesting information on~~ Self-catering cottages in Cumbria. ~~I have pleasure in setting out below details of the accommodation at Calderghyll which is available for the dates which you mentioned.~~

~~A booking form is enclosed for your use and I hope that you will find that you are satisfied with Calderghyll from the details shown.~~ At this time of year many people are making holiday arrangements. ~~and I would suggest that you~~ Telephone our bookings section on 061–763205 as soon as possible in order to make a provisional reservation. You can telephone at any time between 8.00 am and 7.00 pm from Monday to Friday and between 9am ~~10.00 am~~ and 5.00 pm from Saturday to Sunday.

(please change times to 24-hr clock)

✳

The Calderbrook area has two houses wh are available within the dates required.

(indent ½" from left and right margins and change to CAPS)

(Page 2) — make heading same style as 'Self-catering C—— in C——' on Pg 1

CALDERGHYLL (REF CMB424)   Leave 12 clear lines
Calderbrook

This mid-terraced house is near the centre of ~~the town~~ and convenient for all amenities. Luxuriously furnished with antiques and equipped with every labour-saving device, this house offers the ideal place for a relaxing break. Accommodation is for 4 people in 2 twin-bedded rooms on the first floor. The ground floor comprises lounge, kitchen and dining room. The first floor bathroom has both bath and shower.

The owner does not object to one small dog kept under proper control. — Copy to Page 3 in same position under Brockholes.

PRICE BAND 12   NB Available from (correct date inserted for 1st Saturday of next month).

You can be assured
~~I would like to take this opportunity of assuring you~~ of ~~the~~ high standards of service ~~which you can expect~~ from our organisation.   [double line spacing]

We pride ourselves on the careful and thorough processing of enquiries and bookings. All of our properties are regularly inspected and members of staff are available at any time to solve any problems which may arise.

We recommend that you take advantage of our inexpensive insurance cover. The cost is competitive at £4.50 per person per week, and £15.00 for a family (4 ~~to~~ 6 persons).

— move to Pg 1 and insert at *

Page 3

Exercise 3A (continued)

Standardise/ headings throughout
(shoulder)

~~Please contact me if you would like any further information or advice.~~ / I look forward to hearing from you in the near future.

BROCKHOLES COTTAGE (REF CMB 546)

(please leave 15 clear lines here for sketch)

This attractive stone cottage ~~is being~~ *has been* renovated to a very high standard.

It is particularly well-equipped, having an automatic washer, tumble drier, dishwasher & oven. *microwave*

Accom is for 3 or four persons in two bedrooms (one twin, one double). There is a comfortable ~~sitting room~~ *lounge* w a ✓ log fire & a sep kitchen/diner. The modern bathroom has a 3-piece suite and there is a sep. shower room on the ground floor.

The property has the advantages of:

Inset 6 spaces from left
- oil-fired central heating
- electricity for cooking
- private walled garden
- garage for one car

(Copy sentence about dog here)

The cottage is one mile from *shops &* pub, and many clients have already made bookings.
// PRICE BAND 10. NB Available from (2nd Sat of next month).

Use the advanced methods described to move the cursor around the document as you check, proofread and edit Exercise 3A.

3.9 Check that the new page markers are in the correct places on your document.

3.10 Spellcheck your document.

3.11 Proofread your document, comparing it very carefully with the copy. Refer to the notes on consistency of presentation in Unit 2 and *check that you have no inconsistencies* in your work.

3.12 Preview your document, if possible, to make sure that the header and page numbering are present.

3.13 Save your work as **EX3A** but *do not print* your work until you have carried out the global search and replace function in step 3.14.

Global search and replace

Word processing programs can find automatically a given word and exchange it for another given word throughout a document. An example of the way in which this function could be used is a letter being sent out from a school to parents. It would be very easy to produce some letters which referred to **your son** and some which referred to **your daughter** or every occurrence of **he** could be changed to **she**.

On most programs, you can use the search and replace function in two different ways:

    a   You can go straight through the document 'searching and replacing' as requested *without* stopping to confirm every change.

    b   you can instruct the program to stop every time the 'search' word is found to allow you to confirm the change before the word is replaced.

SEARCH AND REPLACE
TEXT GLOBALLY

The latter method is safer and allows you greater control, particularly in examinations. For example, if you replaced the word **son** with the word **daughter** throughout a document using global search and replace without confirmation, a word such as **sonic** could become **daughteric**, and **personal** could become **perdaughteral**!

3.14 The word **bookings** is to be replaced wherever it occurs in Exercise 3A with the word **reservations**. Use the global search and replace function to perform this task.

3.15 Save and print a copy of your work, replacing the old version of **EX3A** with the new version.

Allocation of clear line spaces in double-line spacing

In some programs, it is not possible to leave an even number of clear line spaces within a document by inserting hard returns *if that document is formatted to double-line spacing*.

Experiment on your program – try leaving an *odd* number of clear line spaces and an *even* number of clear line spaces within a piece of text. If your program will not allow you to leave an *even* number of clear line spaces when in double-line spacing, change to single-line spacing immediately after the last word in the first block of text, press *return* the number of times required, then revert to double-line spacing before continuing with the second block of text.

Checking the space between two blocks of text

You can check that you have left the correct amount of clear line spaces simply by placing the cursor in the first clear line space and pressing the ↓ arrow key to move the cursor down one (or two lines) at a time, counting as you go along.

Right alignment of text

LINE SPACING

RIGHT ALIGNMENT OF TEXT

Most programs will allow you to align text at the right margin automatically

LIKE THIS!

Headers, footers and page numbering on one document

In the RSA Stage II and III examinations, you may be asked to insert a header, a footer and page numbering within one document. Make sure these features are *not* set to appear in the same position on a document as they may be printed superimposed on top of each other.

If you are not given definite instructions on the positioning of these features, use your own judgement.

Exercise 3B

3.16 Starting a new document, follow steps 3.1 to 3.4 to set the format for the document:

Header (flush right)	**Shoppers Guide**
Footer (bottom left)	**LETTERS**
Page numbering:	bottom right of every page
Right margin:	ragged or justified
Line spacing:	double-line spacing

3.17 Retrieve your file **EX2B** and follow steps 3.6 and 3.7 to delete unwanted text. (Use the quick methods described earlier in this unit.)

3.18 Amend the text in Exercise 3B as shown, making new pages where you think they should be.

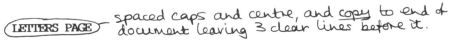

~~LETTERS PAGE~~ — spaced caps and centre, and copy to end of document leaving 3 clear lines before it.

I recently received a request from your organisation for a contribution to your Consumer Information column, which I have pleasure in setting out below.

~~NOT AT ITS BEST?~~ — underline 'A'

There is no reason why you should not buy overdue products because the shopkeeper is obliged to provide goods which meet a certain quality. ~~they must not be "bad" or "off".~~ Even if you (remove indent) buy such goods at a reduced price, your legal rights are not affected. If you are unable to obtain satisfaction from the shop manager, contact the local Trading Standards Officer ~~through~~ at the Town Hall.

Exercise 3B (continued)

Most food producers need to maintain ~~a good~~ *their* reputation and they ~~will usually~~ take ~~any~~ complaints very seriously indeed. It is often a good idea to write to the Managing Director of an organisation enclosing, if possible, a sample of the defective goods. You may have your costs refunded and sometimes a free (gift or sample) is sent to you as a token of goodwill.

~~T S Orwen — (correct date inserted for 1st Friday of next month)~~

You may be
~~It is possible that you are already~~ aware of the fact that ~~it is not unknown for~~ certain people ~~to~~ take advantage of a manufacturer's generosity by frequently returning 'faulty' products. *(However,)* Most manufacturers keep records of these transactions so it is not a practice which I would recommend and it involves ~~more time and~~ effort ~~than it is worth.~~
a lot of / *and expense*

My local shop sometimes sells goods at the end of their 'sell by' date at reduced prices. Is it safe to buy these? | Move para to 'A'

(Indent ½" at left) (single spacing for all 'questions' paras please)

('B')

Although there is considerable expense in postage, some people have almost made a part-time job out of this hobby! Do you think that an extra paragraph to this effect would be useful or relevant for your readers?

Please let me know your decision both on the submitted text and the additional information.

Indent ½" at left [I want to buy good food for my children. Can I bet what the mfrs put on their labels?] single spacing

The 1984 Food Labelling Regulations allowed the public to see exactly what they were eating although some of the names and numbers did not have much meaning.
(leave 4 clear lines)
certain organizations
As a result of pressure from ~~groups~~, many of the unnecessary chemicals have been removed from pre-packed foods & mfrs now (promote actively) the 'wholesome' nature of their goods. /However, as consumers we need to be wary of being fooled by claims such as:

inset by 12 spaces & use single spacing [no added colour
no artificial ingredients
no additives
no preservatives.]

Such
~~These~~ claims may ~~hold~~ *be* true for a product but this does not mean that the ~~food~~ is nutritious. Always read the ingredient list.

Exercise 3B (continued)

FOOD ADDITIVES — Move to 'B'

I hope to hear from you as soon as possible on my article on food additives as you said you may be interested in this.

I enclose my business card so that you may telephone me. I am in full-time employment so you can reach me between the hours of 9.00 am and 5.00 pm at my business number. After 6.00 pm I can be contacted at home.

Pure & Simple?

Flavour is a misleading description — a 'raspberry flavour' food need not contain any raspberry at all!

✓ A 'raspberry flavoured' food shd get a large part of its flavour from raspberries, whereas a 'raspberry' food must be made w whole raspberries. Secret ingredients can creep into some goods. Small amounts of preservatives and sugar do not have to be declared so it is difficult to be sure whether products are really 'pure' and 'natural'.

Some of the descriptions on food labels sound vague, eg 'flavour', 'pure', "natural". What do they really mean?

display this para like other questions ↑

Leave 3 clear lines

Copy heading L— P— here

Operator: please search for 'goods' and replace with 'products' throughout the document

3.19 Spellcheck and proofread your document checking for consistency of presentation.

3.20 Preview your document (if possible) as a final check.

3.21 Save and print a copy of your work. Use the filename **EX3B**.

At the end of Unit 4 you will have

    a   revised all the text-processing theory which you learnt in
Units 1, 2 and 3

    b   revised all the word processing functions on your program
which you learnt in Units 1, 2 and 3.

Exercise 4A

SYNOPSIS OF PRESENTATION

A wide range of everyday things can be turned into wine
and the result are often very palatable and cheap to
produce. Berries, flowers, vegetables, fruits, leaves
and weeds can all be trans formed into into intresting
and colorful drinks.

Many suitable ingrediants can be found in your garden (
or in someone else's) so it is not allways necessary to
visit the greengrocer. You don't need to spend alot of
money on equipment and their are many shops and
supermarkets offering everything you willneed. However,
you must always take grate care in hygiene just as yo
would if you were preparing food.

Available Wenesdays from

Identify the 14 errors in the above passage and key in a correct copy after comparing with handwritten draft. The date to be inserted is 2nd wed of next month. Save as EX4A and print a copy. Change line length to 52 and justify R margin.

SYNOPSIS OF PRESENTATION (bold)

A wide range of everyday things can be turned into wine and the results are often very palatable and cheap to produce. Berries, flowers, vegetables, fruits, leaves and weeds can all be transformed into interesting and colourful drinks.

Many suitable ingredients can be found in your garden (or in someone else's) so it is not always necessary to visit the greengrocer. You don't need to spend a lot of money on equipment and there are many shops and supermarkets offering everything you will need. However, you must always take great care in hygiene just as you would if you were preparing food.

Available Wednesdays from ———

Exercise 4B

> Please key in the letter below, using a ragged right margin.
> Standardise layout and presentation, and retrieve the synopsis
> where indicated (saved as EX4A), restoring line length on retrieved
> text to default settings. Save as EX4B and print a copy.

↗FOR THE A _____ OF THE SPEAKER'S SEC
↳Ref PC/WP/EX4B

Greenbank Centre
Greenbank Lane
DERBY
DE6 7JL

Dr Sirs

WINE-MAKING ← (bold and underline)

I was pleased to rec yr request for a presentation on
the above topic wh I think wd be of interest to members
⊘ of yr ~~club~~ org. A synopsis is given below.

(INSERT TEXT FROM EX4A HERE)

I wd be obliged if you cd let me know the date you wd
prefer asap as I have other organizations regularly
contacting me, & I need a certain amount of time to
make sure that I have a sufficiently wide range of wines
to bring along to a demonstration. A special feature of
my talk is the opp to taste the different wines as well
as being able to take away a copy of the easiest
recipes. I will supply the wine if you will supply
the glasses! I enclose one copy of my Recipes sheet
wh you are welcome to photocopy as necy.

Exercise 4B (continued)

My talk usually lasts for about one hour, followed by approx half an hour for tasting & questions. I could be at yr Centre at 1830 hours. If the talk ~~began~~ ~~commenced~~ at 7.00 pm, I wd anticipate leaving at approx 9 pm. I do not charge a fee but I wd be obliged if you could let me have the token sum of 5 pounds to cover exps.

There are some items of wine making equipment wh I wd like to show you, & I wd need a large table to accommodate these ~~items~~.

Perhaps you could let me have a map and directions if poss to help me to find the G—— Centre. It wd also be of great assistance to me if you could let me know where I can park my car when I arrive. There is quite a lot of carrying to be done both before and after the presentation so the nearer I can ~~drive~~ get to the Centre, the better.

I look forward to hearing from you.

Yrs ffly

PENNY CROFTON (MRS)

Exercise 4C

Retrieve your file EX4B and delete the ref, date, name and address, salutation and complimentary close. Use the header – WINES FROM YOUR GARDEN – at top centre of every page and number the pages at the bottom right. Keep pages as shown, use either ragged or justified right margin and double line-spacing. Save as EX4C and print a copy.

COUNTRY

WINE-MAKING ← spaced caps & centre

I was pleased to receive your request for a presentation on the above topic which I think would be of interest to members of your organisation. A synopsis is given below.

SYNOPSIS OF PRESENTATION   COPY TO ✱

A wide range of everyday things can be turned into wine and the results are often very palatable and cheap to produce.
Berries, flowers, vegetables, fruits, leaves and weeds can all be transformed into interesting and colourful drinks.
(leave 10 clear lines for diagram)
Many suitable ingredients can be found in your garden (or in someone else's) so it is not always necessary to visit the greengrocer. You don't need to spend a lot of money on   Move to
equipment and there are many shops and supermarkets offering   ✱✱
everything you will need. However, you must always take great care in hygiene just as you would if you were preparing food.

Available Wednesdays from (correct date inserted for 2nd Wednesday of next month)

I would be obliged if you could let me know the date you would prefer as soon as possible as I have other organisations regularly contacting me, and I need a certain amount of time to make sure that I have a sufficiently wide range of wines to bring along to a demonstration.

PAGE 1

Exercise 4C (continued)

Basic Facts   (PAGE 2)

During my talk you had
~~A special feature of my talk is~~ the opportunity to taste the
different wines, ~~as well as being able to take away a copy of~~
~~the easiest recipes.~~ ~~I will supply the wine if you will supply~~
~~the glasses! I enclose one copy of~~ My Recipes sheet ~~which you~~
~~are welcome to photocopy as necessary.~~ gives some easy recipes.

My talk usually lasts for about one hour, followed by
approximately half an hour for tasting and questions. I could
be at your Centre is 1830 hours. If the talk began at 1900
hours, I would anticipate leaving at approximately 2100 hours.
I do not charge a fee but would be obliged if you could let me
have the token sum of 5 to cover expenses.

The main stages of wine-making are:
(must 8 spaces and use single spacing with a clear line between items)
1 Extraction of flavour & colour
2 Addition of (ingredients) (other) & fermenting
3 Straining
4 Fermenting
5 Racking
6 Storing – for at least six months
7 Bottling

                                        (NUTRIENT)
Yeast is the most important ingredient in wine-making –
it must be wine yeast – and a yeast nutrient shd be
added.

The main ingredient is the fruit, vegetables,
flowers or herbs wh give the wine its individual
colour, (smell) (and) (taste).
                                                    single spacing

Sugar must be carefully weighed before it is
made into a syrup, and added to the 'must'.
        (, ie dissolved in hot water,)

Exercise 4C (continued)

PAGE 3

← make into a heading

~~There are some items of~~ (wine-making equipment) ~~which I would like to show you, and I would need a large table to accommodate these.~~

~~Perhaps you could let me have directions and a map if possible to help me to find the Greenbank Centre. It would also be of great assistance to me if you could let me know where I can park my car when I arrive. There is quite a lot of carrying to be done both before and after the presentation so the nearer I can get to the Centre, the better.~~

~~I look forward to hearing from you.~~

(single spacing) It is not necy to spend a lot of money on/ ~~equipment~~ special utensils. ✓
You probably have most things in yr kitchen already.
(** ← Move sentence here

Many supermarkets have a range of wine-making equipment and there are specialist shops for the ~~keen~~ enthusiast. Perhaps one of the most helpful aids is yr cellar book where you can record details. (of each wine)

You can have great fun, if you have artistic leanings, in designing your own labels.
(leave 7 clear lines for label diagram)

Any kind of bottle will do for your wine provided it is a <u>wine</u> bottle. Restaurants are usually happy to give away their empties. You will also need:

Indent 1" from left
Corks
bottle brush
siphon hose
corking ~~tool~~
straining cloths
— single spacing —

(*) ← COPY sentence here and put in double spacing.

Change wine-making to country wine-making except in headings

Printing-out arrangements in the RSA Stage II Part 1 examination

You are given 12 sheets of A4 paper in this examination. This is usually sufficient paper to be able to print out *one draft* copy of each task during the examination time and *one final* copy.

The printing of the final copies of the tasks in this examination is done outside the examination time of one-and-one-quarter hours *by the invigilator*.

No amendments may be made to the text after that time has expired and the printing should be done from the directory and files screen.

You are allowed to insert special characters, such as accents, on to the final copies after the examination time.

The invigilator at your examination centre will explain the procedures to be followed for printing in that centre.

Task 1

> Please key in a correct copy of this document.
> There are several errors in the typescript. Refer to
> the manuscript to check as you key in. Use a
> 55-character typing line, and a justified R margin.
> Save as TASK1

RETURNING TO WORK

One of the main concerns facing any one who is
considering returning to work after a few years is the
inability to copy with new technology. This could effect
people in any industry but the revolution in information
technology has perhaps been the greatest chance over a
short period of time. A good retrainning scheme offering
hands-on experiance with up-to-date equipment can help to
to allay some fears and, at the same time, provide the
traines with recognised qualifications in there chosen
vocational area.

Women who have spent some time caring for a family **amy**
lack confidence and assumes that they will have to return
to routine work. It is important that these woman become
able to identify the skills they have aquired so that,
with adequate training and encouragment, they can acheive
their fulll potential and take their place in the world
of work.

RETURNING TO WORK ← (heading only in bold)

One of the main concerns facing anyone who is considering
returning to work after a few years is the inability to cope
with new technology. This could affect people in any industry
but the revolution in information technology has perhaps
been the greatest change over a short period of time. A good
retraining scheme offering hands-on experience with up-to-date
equipment can help to allay some fears and, at the same
time, provide the trainees with recognised qualifications in
their chosen vocational area.

Women who have spent some time caring for a family
may lack confidence and assume that they will have to
return to routine work. It is important that these
women become able to identify the skills they have
acquired so that, with adequate training and
encouragement, they can achieve their full potential
and take their place in the world of work.

Task 2

> Please key in the following letter with a ragged right margin, retrieving the text from Task 1 where shown, and restoring the line length to normal on the retrieved text. Save as TASK 2 and print one copy.

Ref TSD/TRG-WR

For the attention of the ~~Training~~ Personnel Officer

Personnel and Training Department
North East Communications Group
Shield House
Shield Road
NEWCASTLE UPON TYNE
NE6 7YT

Dr Sirs

RECRUITMENT OF/STAFF   (QUALIFIED OFFICE)

I am writing to you as one of the major employers in the area to give you details about the service wh. my company can provide. We were established 5 years ago and have steadily grown so that we now employ six ~~people~~ advisers at our agency in the city centre with 3 ~~employees~~ advisers at our Durham branch. Our special field is the placing of clerical and secretarial staff into both temp & permanent positions and we take considerable care to match our clients with ~~employers~~ workers of the standard requested

Before accepting a potential ~~client~~ employee on to our 'books', we ~~test~~ assess them to ensure that they have the necy aptitude and ability. Educational certificates are checked and the level of current skills is tested ~~by the requirement to take a test~~ on a typewriter or word processor.

Many of the people who come to our agency have not worked for some time and we offer them the opp. to retrain with our parent company, Tyne Training.

> RETRIEVE TASK1 here and delete the heading.

Task 2 (continued)

Tyne Training is ~~in a position~~ able to offer such women the training they need. Programmes are designed to suit individual needs after an initial assessment by qualified advisers. The trainee can brush up on their previous knowledge and skills and have the latest electronic office equipment at their disposal. Women who have not worked in an office environment before take a full programme starting with keyboard skills. Assessment is practical in nature and trainees are reviewed regularly.

[WOOLFORD]

An Information Day is to be held at T— T—'s Woolford Rd Centre on Friday of next week, (please insert date) between 1.00 pm and 7 pm. An invitation and full details are enclosed. Please let me know if you will be able to attend and the number of representatives wh. will be coming from your co. I look forward to meeting you.

Yours sincly
TYNE EMPLOYMENT AGENCY

Tina Davidson
ASSISTANT MANAGER

Task 3

Retrieve your file TASK2 and delete the reference, date, attention line, name and address, salutation and complimentary close. Set a header – TYNE TRAINING – at top right of every page and number pages at bottom centre. Use ragged or justified right margin. Save as TASK3 and print one copy.

TYNE EMPLOYMENT AGENCY
AND
TYNE TRAINING   } centre each line & put in bold

(leave 2 clear lines here)

centre each line

┌ I N F O R M A T I O N   D A Y ← spaced caps
│ Friday ___ ___ from 1.00 pm to 7.00 pm } underline
└ Woolford Rd Centre, Woolford Rd, NE6 5JL

(leave 2 clear lines here)

Copy pg 2+3 * TRAINING TOMORROW'S ~~RECRUITMENT OF QUALIFIED~~ OFFICE STAFF TODAY ← centre & bold

TYNE EMPLOYMENT A_____

~~I am writing to you as one of the major employers in the area to give you details about the service which my company can provide.~~ We were established 5 years ago and have steadily grown so that we now employ 6 advisers at our agency in the city centre with 3 advisers at our Durham branch. Our special field is the placing of clerical and secretarial staff into both temporary and permanent positions and we take considerable care to ~~match~~ provide our clients with workers of the standard requested.

Before accepting a potential employee ~~on to our 'books'~~, we } Indent
assess them to ensure that they have the necessary aptitude | 1" at
and ability. Educational certificates are checked and the | each
level of current skills is tested on a typewriter or word | side
processor.

TYNE TRAINING
Many of the people who come to our agency have not worked for some time and we offer them the opportunity to retrain with our parent company, Tyne Training.

(Office)
One of the main concerns facing anyone who is considering returning to work after a few years is the inability to cope with new technology. ~~This could affect people in any industry but the revolution in information technology has perhaps been the greatest change over a short period of time.~~ A good retraining scheme offering hands-on experience with up-to-date equipment can help to allay some fears and, at the same time, provide the trainees with recognised qualifications in their chosen vocational area.

~~Women who have spent some time caring for a family may lack confidence and assume that they will have to return to routine work.~~ It is important that ~~these~~ women (become able to) (returners) identify the skills they have ~~acquired~~ so that, with adequate training and encouragement, they can achieve their full potential and take their place in the world of work.

Task 3 (continued)

(PAGE 2)

Tyne Training is able to offer such women the training they
need. Programmes are designed to suit individual needs after
an initial assessment by qualified advisers. The trainees can
brush up on their previous knowledge and skills and have the
latest electronic office equipment at their disposal. Women
who have not worked in an office environment before take a
full programme starting with keyboard skills. Assessment is
(each) practical in nature and trainees are reviewed regularly. (progress is)

An Information Day is to be held at Tyne Training's Woolford
Road Centre on Friday of next week, between 1.00 pm and
7.00 pm. An invitation and full details are enclosed. Please
let me know if you will be able to attend and the number of
representatives which will be coming from your company. I
look forward to meeting you.

When we are satisfied that a trainee has reached | Move
a good level of ability, we assist him or her to find | to end
work. Specialist tutors guide trainees through the | of this
process of looking for a suitable position, preparing | page
for an interview, (applying for the post) and finally | at
getting through the actual interview successfully | **

Our training ~~courses~~ programmes are designed to accommodate
individual needs. The 'core' curriculum covers:-
(Indent 1" at left)
1 Text processing skills
2 Administrative procedures
3 Electronic office

Options may be added from the following list
after initial assessment:

Indent | Shorthand
½" at | Audio-typewriting
left & | French for the Office
double-spacing

Please change
'trainee(s)'
to 'student(s)'
throughout task.

**

(* Copy heading here from Page 1)

38

Task 3 (continued)

(PAGE 3)

Copy headings from Page 1
to here —(TYNE EMPLOYMENT
to Woolford Rd, NE6 5JL)

Double-
spacing for
this page

LOOKING FOR THE BEST STAFF?

Tyne Training's Woolford Rd Centre will
be open to visitors from commerce &
industry. If you are interested in
recruiting first-class personnel, call
in and see our trainees at work.
You'll be impressed by their efficiency
and the wide range of skills they have
at their fingertips!

Leave 9 clear lines for map & logo

LOOKING FOR THE BEST TRAINING?

The Tyne Training Centre can help you.
Ask about our wide range of
'personalised' programmes, free training
and excellent results. See the trainees
in action.   Ask them about the Centre—
they are our best ~~adverts~~ advocates!

SPECIALIST STAFF WILL BE AVAILABLE TO DEAL WITH] single
YOUR QUERIES ON RECRUITMENT OR TRAINING   ] spacing

Refreshments provided

* Copy heading here from Page 1

At the end of Unit 6 you will have learnt how to:

    a   complete a form with given information
    b   insert relevant details at appropriate entry points using the search facility.

In the Stage II examination, the form will already have been keyed in for you. For the purposes of this book, however, you will have to key in the form(s) yourself.

When completing forms, you will be given the details to be entered at appropriate points on the form. The details may not be supplied in the same order, however, as the sequence of headings on the form.

It is important, therefore, that you check the information carefully and match it up against each heading requiring completion.

If the same form is to be used frequently, you can store the form layout as a 'master' or 'skeleton' on your word processing system and retrieve it to screen whenever you need to enter details at preset points.

The preset points at which details are to be inserted are often referred to as 'entry points' – see the next section.

Entry points

To complete a given form on the word processor you can operate a search command to locate 'entry points'. Entry points are simply marked (preset) points at which relevant information is to be inserted against a heading or item. The entry point is usually denoted by a symbol which does not normally appear in the text, e.g., $, *, #, etc. After searching for the entry-point symbol, you should delete it and then insert the relevant piece of information in its place.

Remember to look carefully at the content of the text you are presented with. It will be up to you to use your initiative to extract the appropriate information required for insertion on to the form.

Your style of presentation should be consistent, unless it is specified otherwise. All other entries may be done in CAPITALS if you wish.

If you are entering information which is to take up more than one line, e.g., an address, you will first need to set a tab in place of the entry point so that the lines begin at the same point:

If the form shows: **Address: @**
Search for and **delete** the @
Set a left-aligned tab at the point where the @ sign was positioned.
Key in the address, using the tab setting to position the start of each address line.

The form will now show: Address: **45 Ridings Lane**
                                    Suftborough
                                    LEEDS

Allocate vertical space

In single-line spacing: 6 clear lines = 1 inch.

(Remember to turn up an extra line space to leave a given measurement clear.)

10 characters = 1 inch (10 pitch)

12 characters = 1 inch (12 pitch)

Note: Remember to change right margin to allocate space at right of document

Blocked capitals

Press: Caps lock key

Centre text

To centre text before keying in:

To centre text already keyed in:

To remove centring:

Change logged disk drive to A:

Clear the screen

Copy block of text

Create a new document

Cursor movement

Move cursor to required position	Use the arrow keys (cursor keys) $\longrightarrow$ $\longleftarrow$ $\downarrow\uparrow$ to move cursor to required position.
Move to start/end of document	**Press:** Home Home $\uparrow$ or Home Home $\downarrow$
Move left/right word by word	**Press:** Ctrl + $\longleftarrow$ or Ctrl + $\longrightarrow$
Move to start/end of line	**Press:** Home + $\longleftarrow$ or Home + $\longrightarrow$
Move to top/bottom of screen	**Press:** Home $\uparrow$ or Home $\downarrow$
Move to top of previous page	
Move to top of next page	
Move cursor to specified page	**Press:** Ctrl + Home **Type:** No. of page required $\longleftarrow\!\lrcorner$

Deleting text

Delete a character	Move cursor to incorrect character. **Press:** Del *or* Move cursor to right of incorrect character. **Press:** $\longleftarrow$ (Del)
Delete to end of line	
Delete to end of page	
Delete to end of sentence	
Delete a word	
Delete word left of cursor	
Delete word right of cursor	
Delete a block of text	

Edit text – delete and insert

Delete character(s)   Move cursor to incorrect character.

Press: Del (delete key)   or

Move cursor to right of incorrect character.

Press: ⟵ (backspace delete key)

Delete a word

Replace text by 'overtyping'   Move cursor to incorrect entry.
(typeover)   Press: Ins key (typeover on)

Overtype with correct entry.

Press: Ins key (typeover off)

Insert characters or words   Position cursor where missing characters

should be inserted:

Key in the missing character(s) or word(s)

Existing text will 'move over' to make room

for the new text.

Embolden text

To embolden text before
keying in:

To embolden text already
keyed in:

To remove bold:

Entry points

To set up:

To search for:

(Use typeover mode if there is more that one entry point on the line. Remember to
align entry points with a tab setting for information going on to more than one line.)

Exit the program

Footers

Footer with automatic
page numbering:

Footnotes

Use asterisk(s) e.g., *, **, *** or superscripted
number [3] to enter footnote(s) in body of text
(no space before footnote symbol).

Leave one space after explanatory footnote
symbol(s) at bottom of passage/document.

Headers

Help function

Indent function

To indent at left margin:

To indent at left and
right margin:

Insert text

Simply key in the missing character(s) at the
appropriate place – the existing text will
'move over' to make room for the new text.

Justified right margin

Key in text

Line length – to change to fixed length

You can fit 82 characters across A4 paper using 10-pitch. If the left and right margins are set to 1 inch, then there are 62 characters across the typing line.

To reduce this to a 'fixed' length:

(1) add all the required characters to left margin

(2) add all the required characters to right margin

(3) add some of required characters to left margin and some to right.

Line spacing

Logged drive (to change)

Margins (to change)

Move block of text

New page marker

Page numbering

Suppress page numbering on current page:

Paragraphs – splitting/joining

Make a new paragraph i.e. split an existing paragraph into two	Move cursor to first letter of new paragraph. **Press:** ←⏎ twice
Join two consecutive paragraphs into one	Move cursor to first character of second paragraph.
	Press: ←— Del twice (backspace delete key)
	Press: Spacebar (to insert space(s)) after full stop

Pitch (to change)

Print out hard copy

Check that the printer is switched on, is 'on-line' and has paper in it.

Ragged right margin

Remove text emphasis

Replace text – typeover

Move cursor to incorrect entry. **Press:** Ins key (typeover on). Overtype with correct entry. **Press:** Ins key (typeover off).

Restore deleted text

Retrieve a file

Right alignment of text

Save work to disk

Search and replace text globally

Search for text

Search forward:

Search backward:

Repeat search:

Shade a block of text

Sort, by line

To sort in descending order:

Spaced capitals

Press: Caps lock key
Leave one space after each letter.
Leave three spaces after each word.

Spellcheck

Standard paragraphs

Switch on and load WP program

Tabulation

Set a new tab:

Left-aligned tab:

Right-aligned tab:

Decimal tab:

Delete individual tab setting:

Change the position of tab setting:

Delete all tab settings together:

Reset tabs at regular settings:

Underline text

To underline text before keying in:

To underline text already keyed in:

To remove underline:

View document

View file directory

Widow/orphan protection

Typeover mode in form entry

Where there are two entry points on the same line, you may have to put typeover mode on (the **Ins Key**). This will allow you to insert the information at the first entry point on the line without pushing the second one out of place, although it may appear to do so when you first key in the text. However, when you move to the next entry point, it should 'jump' back into place.

(If the second item has been set and reached by using a tab setting, it 'jumps' back into place – if the spacebar is used, it is pushed out when text is entered.)

Search facility

You can use your program to search through your document forwards or backwards, enabling you to locate quickly any string of word(s) or character(s) (or CODES) wherever they appear. You can use the search facility to locate entry points.

SEARCH FOR TEXT

Exercise 6A

6.1 Starting a new document, key in the form below following the layout exactly as shown and using the @ sign to represent the entry point. Delete all existing tabs. Set a left-aligned tab at 40 (for the **Tel No** entry). Save your work – use the filename **Form6A**.

```
                   BRITANNIA BULBS ORDER FORM
                          26 Rocks Road
                            Sheffield
                             S4 7JB


        Customer Name: @

        Address: @

        Post Code: @                Tel No: @

        Bulbs Type: @

        Variety: @

        Cat No: @

        Quantity: @

        Price: @

        Date of Order: @

        Method of Payment: @

        _____

        TO BE COMPLETED BY DESPATCH DEPARTMENT

        Despatch Date .......... Despatched by ...............
```

Exercise 6B

6.2   Starting a new document, key in the form below following the lay out exactly as shown and using the $ sign to represent the entry point. Delete all existing tabs. Set a left-aligned tab at 55 (for the **Branch No** and **To** entries). Save your work – use the filename **Form6B**.

```
W H BRIDGES & CO
SALES PROMOTION – WEEKEND RESIDENTIAL

PERSONNEL ACCOMMODATION DETAILS

Branch: $                              Branch No: $

Branch Tel No: $

No of Personnel attending: $
Name(s) of Personnel: $

Date of Residential: From: $                 To: $

Accommodation required: $

Attendance confirmed on (date): $
```

Exercise 6C

6.3   Starting a new document, retrieve the file **FORM6A**. To complete the form use the search facility to locate each occurrence of the @ entry point. Delete the @, then extract the relevant information from the letter below and insert in its place.

Save and print a copy of your work – use the filename **EX6C**.

```
Woodnook Cottage
Woodnook Close
BRADFORD   BD5 TR2
Tel No: 0274 384572

15 July 1993

Dear Sir/Madam

I would like to place an order with you for 3 dozen Tulips
(Queen Alicia variety) priced at £2.35 per dozen. The
catalogue number is TU3782. I enclose a cheque to cover cost
of Tulips and packaging.

Yours faithfully

J Smithies

J Smithies (Mrs)
```

Exercise 6D

6.4 Starting a new document, retrieve the file **FORM6A** again and complete the form, this time using the information given in the telephone message below.

Save and print a copy of your work – use the filename **EX6D**.

TELEPHONE MESSAGE

FROM: Walter Riley   TO: Sales Department
4 Bridge Lane
Huddersfield
HD2 8FL Tel No: 0484 37625

MESSAGE:

Mr Riley rang to order 5 dozen crocus bulbs, cat no CR 2212 @ £1.50 per dozen. He wants the Mixed Variety and has paid in full by VISA

RECEIVED BY: Kate Davies DATE: 16 July 1992

Exercise 6E

6.5 Starting a new document, retrieve the file **FORM6B** and complete the form using the information given in the memorandum below.

Save and print a copy of your work – use the filename **EX6E**.

M E M O R A N D U M

From   Chris Blanchard, Manager
Ref: LEEDS Branch No 346

To: Head Office

Date: 27 July 1993

RE: WEEKEND RESIDENTIAL – SALES PROMOTION

I am pleased to confirm that 2 members of staff will be able to attend the weekend residential sales promotion. One will be myself and the other is my assistant, Diane Whitely.

We will require overnight accommodation for 2nd and 3rd of August 1993 – 2 single rooms with bath please.

Can you ring me at the Branch Tel No (0532 683462) asap with travel details.

At the end of Unit 7 you will have learnt how to:

    a   set up standard paragraphs

    b   retrieve standard paragraphs into a document.

You will need to refresh your memory on

    c   the conventions of business letter layout

    d   changing your right margin or indenting text from the right.

Standard letters

Many letters have some parts in them that are identical in content. This can mean keying in the same portions of text over and over again, e.g., company addresses, standard paragraphs or the salutation at the end.

You can store these standard portions of text as separate files and then retrieve them as required into any document. This can obviously save you a great deal of keying-in time. It is sometimes called 'boilerplating'.

Your standard letter needs to be well displayed. In the Stage II examination you must standardize on layout, line spacing and heading styles. You will need to emphasize text (bold, underline, etc.) and extract information from another task. Also, don't forget to insert the date in the correct position.

To set up standard paragraphs

    1   Key in the text for each pargraph (or portion of text).

    2   Save each paragraph (or portion of text, as a separate file in the usual way. If you use easily identifiable filenames it will help you to retrieve the correct file, e.g., **SINCE** for a **Yours sincerely** closure, or **FAITH** for a **Yours faithfully** closure.

To retrieve the standard paragraph

    1   Position the cursor at the place you want the text to be inserted.

RETRIEVE A FILE

    2   Operate the command appropriate to your system for retrieving a standard (paragraph) file.

Exercise 7A

7.1 Starting a new document, key in the following standard paragraphs, saving (or creating) each one with the filename indicated at the left.

Filename

ADDRESS
```
BRITANNIA BULBS
26 Rocks Road
Sheffield
S4 7JB

Tel No: 0742 472831
```

ORDER
```
Thank you for your recent order for a selection of
our bulbs.
```

ENQUIRY
```
Thank you for your recent enquiry regarding a
selection of our bulbs.
```

INSTOCK
```
We are pleased to advise you that these items are in
stock and should arrive within the next fourteen
days.
```

OUTSTOCK
```
We are sorry to advise you that these items are
currently out of stock.
```

PRICE
```
Please find enclosed an up-to-date price list and
this season's brochure.
```

SINCE
```
Yours sincerely
BRITTANIA BULBS



Sales Department
```

FAITH
```
Yours faithfully
BRITTANIA BULBS



Sales Department
```

Exercise 7B

7.2   Starting a new document, key in the letter below with a ragged right margin. As you key in the letter, retrieve the relevant standard paragraphs using the filenames shown (e.g., **ADDRESS**) at the appropriate marked points.

Save and print your work – use the filename **EX7B**.

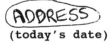 (ADDRESS)

```
(today's date)

Mrs J Smithies
Woodnook Cottage
Woodnook Close
BRADFORD   BD5 2TR

Dr Mrs Smithies

Re your order of 15 July 1992
```
please emphasise this heading

(ORDER)

```
Our records show yr order was for: 3 dozen Tulips, Queen
Alicia variety          at a cost of (refer to Exercise 4.3 for this
information) per dozen.
```

(INSTOCK)

```
A rec for your cheque will be enclosed w the bulbs, along with

instructions for planting. We look forward to hearing from you

again.
```

(SINCE)

Follow the line spacing of the paragraph beginning "Our records ____"

Exercise 7C

7.3 Starting a new document, key in the letter below with a justified right margin. Retrieve the relevant standard paragraphs at the points shown.

Save and print your work – use the filename **EX7C**.

(ADDRESS)

please emphasise the words underlined with a ~~~~

Mr Walter Riley
4 Bridge Lane
HUDDERSFIELD
HD2 FL8

Dear Mr Riley

(ORDER)

Our re cords show that your order was for 5 Mixed dozen Crocus bulbs, Cat No CR2212, and that you have already paid in full by (refer to Ex 4.4 for payment type).

(OUTSTOCK) In fact, your order was taken from a cat which was out-of-date. (PRICE)

(alternative) We will be pleased to supply you with an optional selection from the new cat or offer you a full refund.

leave a space here 2" across by 1" down (51mm × 25mm) for a voucher

Please accept our apologies for any incon caused, along with the attached 50p voucher.

(SINCE)

Encs

all text to start from left margin as in the paragraph which begins "Our records show ....."

47

Exercise 7D

7.4 Starting a new document, key in the letter below with a ragged right margin. Retrieve the relevant standard paragraphs at the points shown.

Save and print your work – use the filename **EX7D**.

(ADDRESS)

```
H Jones & Son
Beaver Works
Drye Rd
HALIFAX
HX4 8UY
```

Dr Sirs

(ENQUIRY)

make all paragraphs the same style as the first one

plans
We are pleased to hear of your ~~intentions~~ to improve the firm's car-parking area with shrubbery ~~and~~ bulbs, and ~~and~~ wd like to take this opp to tell you about our new Garden Helpline Service.

Details of this are explained in the accompanying leaflet, along with our ~~our~~ new Gardener's Helpline Telephone Number. When returning your order form, could you please let us know where you saw our advert as this will assist our marketing dept.

(PRICE)

(FAITH)

please use any word processing method to give prominence to the words underlined with mmm

Encs

7.5 Exit the program if you have finished working or continue straight on to the next unit.

At the end of Unit 8 you will have learnt how to:

a　enter footnotes
b　rearrange table items in a specified order
c　adapt a table to fit on the specified paper size
d　alter the pitch size
e　work out tab settings for an advanced table display.

In the RSA Stage II examination, the table task contains a number of additional features to the tabulation work you completed at Stage I. You should refresh your memory on editing and tabulation procedures.

Since the table is usually quite large, you will also need to give consideration to making it fit on the page/paper size being used. If you think the table won't quite fit using your normal settings, there are several options open to you:

● reduce the left and right margins to $^1/2$ inch – this is the least amount acceptable
● wrap the text around on to the next line in the column
● reduce the size of the pitch – see the section below on changing the pitch size.

Working out tab-setting positions for advanced table display

Your program will probably have tab stops positioned evenly across the typing line, usually at every $^1/2$ inch. It is often possible simply to use these default tab settings for most column work. (Remember to allow sufficient room for the longest line in each column.)

If the table is too large to fit on the page using the default tab settings, you will need to consider the following options:

Option 1

Alter the pitch size to 12 CPI (see the section on changing the pitch size).

Option 2

Reduce the margin settings to $^1/2$ inch. It is seldom necessary to make both of these changes.

If necessary, make any changes to pitch or margins *before* setting the tabs.

There is sometimes one column that is variable in width – it can be made narrower if the text is narrative in style (i.e., text 'runs on' and is not made up of separate items) by putting the text on to more than one line. This means it may not be necessary to change the pitch size or the margins.

Typing line

When calculating the amount of 'character space' across an A4 page, note the following:

- If you are using 10-pitch CPI with left and right margin settings of 1 inch, your right margin will be at 72 and you will have 62 character spaces across the page.
- If you are using 10-pitch CPI with left and right margin settings at $1/2$ inch, your right margin will be at 77 and you will have 72 character spaces across the page.
- If you are using 12-pitch CPI with left and right margin settings of 1 inch, your right margin will be at 87 and you will have 76 character spaces across the page.

Ruler line

If your program has a ruler line, bring this up to check your margins and tab stops.

Setting your tabs

Enter the tab menu and delete all existing tab settings. Set tabs appropriate for the table task in hand. The type of data in the table will determine whether you should:

- work backwards from the right margin to set the tabs
- work forwards from the left margin to set the tabs
- use a combination of these two methods if the variable width column is not at the extreme left or right of the table.

As a general rule, where you have a 'variable column' (i.e., a column containing text and leader dots, or with 'narrative' text which can sensibly run on to more than one line) it is easier to set tabs to mark the columns of 'fixed' width first.

You should work forwards from the left margin (method 1) until you reach the variable column. You should then work backwards from the right margin (method 2) until you reach the variable column from the other direction. The space that is left after you have done this is automatically allocated to the variable column (there is no need to calculate a specific number of characters).

If the table does not contain leader dots, and all the column entries are meant to fit on to one line, you should space forwards from the left margin (method 1).

Method one   Position cursor at the left margin on ruler line in the tab-set menu. Press the right arrow key once for every character in the longest line of the first column, plus an extra three times for the space between the first and second columns. (Don't forget to check the column heading – it may be longer than the items in the column itself.) Set a left-aligned tab.

Repeat the procedure for the number of characters in the longest line of the second column plus three for the space, and set a second tab. Continue in this way for all the column tab settings in the table.

Method two   Position cursor at the right margin on ruler line in the tab-set menu. Press the left arrow key once for every character in the longest line of the last column. (Don't forget to check the column heading – it may be longer than the items in the column itself.) Set a left-aligned tab.

Move to the left three times for the space between the columns, then press the left arrow key once for every character in the longest line of the next-to-last column and set a left-aligned tab.

Keying in the table

Exit the tab menu if you have set new tabs, and return to your document. You can check that you have set the correct number of tabs if you have a ruler-line facility on your system.

TABULATION

Use the tab key to move between the columns and enter the appropriate information into each column.

Subdivided and multi-line column headings

If the copy you are working from shows subdivided or multi-line column headings, remember to include these in your calculations for working out the tab settings.

A multi-line column heading means that the column heading appears on more than one line:

COURSE	START DATE	END DATE	COST
(col 1)	(col 2)	(col 3)	(col 4)

A sub-divided column heading means that the column heading may be divided into two or more subheadings:

COURSE	COURSE DATES START END	COST
(col 1)	(col 2)	(col 3)

Changing the pitch size

If you have a lot of information to fit on the page, you may need to change the size of the pitch. Word processors usually use 10-pitch (10 CPI – characters per inch) by default. Most word processing programs have a facility which will allow you to select a smaller pitch size such as 12-pitch (12 CPI) – this will enable you to fit more data on to the table.

PITCH (to change)

Your table should either be all in 10-pitch or all in 12-pitch – not a mixture!

Footnotes

A footnote is a piece of information placed at the end of each page (or document) which explains, in more depth, a particular point made within the body of the text.

A footnote symbol, such as a *, is placed in the body of the text next to the point which needs further explanation. The same symbol is repeated at the end of the page or document with the explanatory text next to it. If more than one footnote is needed, you can use two asterisks – e.g., **.

There is no space *before* the footnote symbol in the body of the text.

There is at least one space *between* the footnote symbol and the explanatory text at the end of the page/document.

Note: This is a simple, manual method of footnote entry. Many word processing programs offer a more sophisticated facility for entering footnotes but the authors feel this is not necessarily appropriate for students at intermediate level. However, you may consult your user manual or your tutor if you wish.

Exercise 8A

8.1 Starting a new document, enter the following table for BRITTANIA BULBS – it will fit on an A4 page in 10-pitch:

   a Delete the existing tab settings. Then enter left-aligned tab settings for the column headings at **48**, **57**, **65**.

   b Key in main headings and column headings of the table, **BRITTANIA BULBS** to **SPRING FLOWERING** inclusive.

   c You now need to change:

     ● the **CAT NO** tab setting to a leader-dot tab (so the entries will be preceded by a row of leader dots)
     ● the **PRICE** tab setting to a decimal tab (so the figures in the price column will wrap around the decimal point).

   d Key in the first entry for column 1: **CROCUS – Purple delight** – press the space bar once, then press the tab key to move to the second column.

   e Key in the entry for column 2: **CR2213. Press** the tab key to move to the third column. Key in the price: **1.65**. Note how the figures automatically wrap around the decimal tab. Press the tab key and enter the data for the final **UNIT** column: **dozen**.

   f Repeat the above procedure for each row.

   g Refer back to the instructions given previously for entering footnotes.

   h Save your work – using the filename **EX8A**. Don't print out at this stage.

```
BRITTANIA BULBS

LATEST ADDITIONS TO THE CATALOGUE:

BULB DESCRIPTION                       CAT NO    PRICE    UNIT

SPRING FLOWERING

CROCUS – Purple Delight   . . . . . .  CR2213     1.65    dozen
TULIP – Princess Orange Maiden . . .   TU3784     3.50    dozen
IRIS – Lilac Lady   . . . . . . . .    IRI21      2.40    dozen
ANENOME – Rainbow Palette   . . . . .  AN8167     4.55    fifty
SPECIAL SPRING MIXTURE*   . . . . . .  SB14      10.00    hundred

AUTUMN FLOWERING

GLADIOLUS – White Heat  . . . . . . .  GL36       0.75    three
ZEPHYRANTHES – Autumn Breeze   . . . . ZE13       0.45    each
ACIDANTHERA   – Princess Rhia   . . .  AC3334     0.95    each
SPECIAL AUTUMN MIXTURE  . . . . . . .  SB14      15.00    hundred

* Also available in Units of 500 at a Discount Price of £35.00
```

Rearranging the table items

In the RSA Stage II examination, you will be asked to rearrange or sort the table into a particular order. There are several ways to do this. The choice is yours.

Method 1 Before you begin to key in the table, use a piece of scrap paper to note down, in advance, the order in which the entries should be keyed in.

Method 2 Key in the entries as they are displayed, then use block and move functions to rearrange the items in the required order.

Method 3 Key in the entries as they are displayed, then if your program has a line-sort facility, use this to sort the items into the required order. To use line sort, the data must usually be set out in rows and columns. You can choose to sort alphabetically (A–Z), or numerically (0, 1, 2, 3, 4…). Therefore, line sort is only effective if all entries on the table take up one line only, otherwise secondary lines will be included in the sort.

SORT, BY LINE

Exercise 8B

8.2 Retrieve the file **EX8A** if it is not already on your screen. You are now going to rearrange the items in alphabetical order of **BULB DESCRIPTION**. However, you must keep the **SPRING FLOWERING** and **AUTUMN FLOWERING** sections separate.

As you have already entered the data for this exercise, you could not predetermine the order while keying in. Use block and move methods or, if your program has the facility, try out line sort.

8.3 Now, try sorting the table into numeric order of **PRICE**. Again, keep the **SPRING FLOWERING** and **AUTUMN FLOWERING** sections separate.

8.4 Save and print your work – use the filename **EX8B**.

Exercise 8C

8.5 Starting a new document, key in the table below. You can key it in using 10-pitch and reduce the left and right margin settings to ½ inch – your right margin will then be at 77. (You do not need to use leader dots.)

Please emphasize the words marked by ✕

Save and print your work – use the filename **EX8C**.

W H BRIDGES & CO SALES PROMOTION ← (centre)

WEEKEND RESIDENTIAL (to the attendance list)

The personnel following are to be directly involved with the company's new sales promotion scheme. Their names need to be added for the weekend residentials to be held in ~~July~~ August

DETAILS OF BRANCHES		PAYROLL	NAME	DATE OF
NO	NAME	NO		W/R*
346	LEEDS	24671	DIANE WHITELY	3/8/92
346	LEEDS	23672	CHRIS BLANCHARD	3/8/92
311	BRADFORD	37268	ASHRAF AKBAR	10/8/92
314	SHEFFIELD	37283	MAVIS RAWSON	10/8/92
311	BRADFORD	28473	MARGARET SUNCLIFFE	10/8/92
237	YORK	27346	SUSANNAH BLAKELY	17/8/92
~~237~~	~~YORK~~	~~22366~~	~~IRENE STEAD~~	~~17/8/92~~
237	YORK	18384	CHRISTOPHER BLAND	17/8/92
119	HUDDERSFIELD	36272	STEPHAN ITRYCH	24/9/92
119	HUDDERSFIELD	27474	MARTIN HOLROYD	24/8/92

* The Weekend Residentials start on the dates listed in the above table but a number of personnel will require an overnight stay the previous night – details of these to follow shortly.

retain date entries in the format shown

please re-arrange the table in alphabetical order of surname

54

Exercise 8D

8.6　Starting a new document, key in the table below. Alter the pitch to 12-pitch to make the table fit on an A4 page with the shorter edge at the top – you may keep left and right margins set at 1 inch.

Please emphasize words marked by a 〰〰〰

Don't forget to use a *decimal tab setting* for the last column.

Save and print your work – use the filename **EX8D**.

> *please re-arrange the table in alphabetical order of ITEM DESCRIPTION*

MUSIC PROMOTIONS LTD

SPECIAL OFFERS

special

> *leave a space here at least 2" across and ½" down (51mm × 13mm) for a stamp*

We are pleased to announce this month's /offers. All units are supplied in ash\black effect finish. Special discounts on bulk orders (twenty-five or more). *(are available)*

ITEM DESCRIPTION	SIZE	CAT NO	PRICE
REGENT 3-drawer ~~compact disc~~ *audio cassette* storage cabinet	14x12x7 in	ZX235	14.99
DEXCEL 2-drawer compact disc storage unit	13x5x16 in	WR114	5.25
~~KORA 3-drawer record storage case~~	~~16x16x14 in~~	~~WT223~~	~~7.99~~
STAVER 4-drawer compact disc library cabinet	12x12x7 in	WR256	12.99
XENON de-luxe audio cassette storage case*	7x7x11 in	ZX551	5.49
NEWSTYLE cassette carousel	7x7x10 in	ZX727	3.99

* This item also /in luxury, green leather‿-look vinyl. *available*

8.7　Exit the program if you have finished working or continue straight on to the next unit.

Exercise 9A

Key in the following form exactly as shown below. Save under filename **EX9A** then clear your screen.

```
THE THREE EAGLES HOTEL

WEDDING RECEPTION BOOKING FORM

NAME $
ADDRESS $
TEL NO $

NO OF GUESTS          ROOM REQUIRED
$                     $

RECEPTION DATE        RECEPTION TIME
$                     $


TYPE OF CATERING REQUIRED
$

COST OF ROOM          COST OF CATERING (per head)
$                     $

DEPOSIT PAID          DATE
$                     $
```

Exercise 9B

Retrieve the file **EX9A** and complete the form with the appropriate information from the message below.

Save and print your work – use the filename **EX9B**.

Message for Hotel Manager

Susan Bailey of 2 Grandesmere Place, Manchester, called into Reception and left a £50 deposit for the Atlantic Room. She wants to book the room for 150 guests for her wedding reception on Sep 12 between 1.30pm & 4.30pm. We have made a provisional booking for the room at a charge of £55 and £7.50 per head for the CARVERY catering. Can you ring Susan on 061-4782001 to confirm the booking ASAP.

Mary Saville (Receptionist)
18 July

Exercise 9C

Key in the following standard paragraphs. Save each one under the filename shown.

Filename

EAGLES   THE THREE EAGLES HOTEL
4 Grandways Road
MANCHESTER   MN4 ET2

CONFIRM   I am pleased to confirm the provisional booking for
your

MENU   Please find enclosed some sample menus of all our
catering options.

MAP   I hope the attached map of the Three Eagles location
will be of help to any guests travelling to your
reception from other areas.

BEST   Best wishes

Jane Lumb (MANAGERESS)

Exercise 9D

Key in the letter below with a justified right margin. Recall the relevant paragraphs and insert at the points marked.

Save and print your work – use the filename **EX9D**.

(EAGLES)
(today's date)

Miss Susan Bailey
2 Grandsmere Place
MANCHESTER

Dear Susan

WEDDING RECEPTION

use the same style for all the headings, following the style of the last one, ACCOMMODATION

(CONFIRM)   wedding reception to take place on,
(refer to Con 2b for the date to insert here)

          CATERING

I bel. you have requested CARVERY-style catering @ £7.50 per head. As an alternative, you may wish to consider our cold and hot Buffet menus. (MENU)

Room

                                                    comfortably
You have been allocated the ATLANTIC ROOM which will hold between 125–160 guests and will therefore accommodate your present guest list.

                    5
A fixed charge of £5 is payable for the room.

Shd. you find you need to cater for additional guests, we can offer a larger room at no extra cost providing you notify us within the next month.

ACCOMMODATION

I understand you have relatives attending the function who wish to book an overnight stay at the Hotel. Please send us details of any requirements as soon as possible.

I shall contact you again in due course to make final arrangements.
(BEST)

please emphasise all the headings

Encs

Exercise 9E

Key in the table below. You may alter the line length or pitch if necessary to make it fit on an A4 page with the shorter end at the top.

Save and print your work – use the filename **EX9E**.

THE THREE EAGLES   ⎫ centre
4 Grandways Road
MANCHESTER   MN4 ET2 ⎭

FUNCTION BOOKINGS – SEPTEMBER ← *use a form of emphasis for this heading*

Hotel rooms have ~~been~~ (temporary) booked for the following dates in September. Please arrange for staff to be contracted for all events, but particularly where there are ~~a lot of guests~~ / high guest numbers.

leave a space at least 2" across by 1" down (51mm x 25mm) for hotel logo

CLIENT NAME	MENU	COST (£) PER HEAD	GUEST NOS	DATE BOOKED
Betty Walsden	CARVERY	£7.50	100	26 SEP
Sebastian MacIntosh	COLD BUFFET	£5.50	145	22 SEP
Susan Bailey	CARVERY	£7.50	155	12 SEP
~~Denise Watson~~	~~CARVERY~~	~~£7.50~~	~~145~~	~~12 SEP~~
Anabella Ferrybridge	HOT BUFFET	£6.50	60	13 SEP
David Ridgeway	COLD BUFFET	£5.50	85 100	20 SEP
Margaret Helm	CARVERY	£7.50	~~110~~	2 SEP
Mohammed Zafar	HOT BUFFET	£6.50	125	8 SEP
Henry Swan	CHEESE/WINE	£4.75*	50	18 SEP

* Cost per head conditional on ~~numbers attending and~~ available house wines.

please re-arrange the table in order of DATE BOOKED starting with the beginning of the month

operator: retain the abbreviations for the months

Printing-out arrangements

Printing-out arrangements in the RSA Stage II Part 2 examination

You are given sufficient paper to be able to print out one draft copy of each task during the examination time.

The printing of the final copies of the tasks in this examination is done outside the examination time of one-and-one-quarter hours *by the candidate*.

No amendments may be made to the text after that time has expired and the printing should be done from the list files (or Directory) screen. (*There is no need to retrieve the document to print.*)

You are allowed to insert special characters, such as accents, on to the final copies after the examination time.

The invigilator at your examination centre will explain the procedures to be followed for printing in that centre.

Task 4

Key in the following form exactly as shown below. Save under the filename
TASK4. (Use the copy below as a print-out check.)

```
TYNE EMPLOYMENT AGENCY
NEWCASTLE UPON TYNE

APPLICANT DETAILS

Name: &

Address: &

Tel No:    Home: &
           Work: &

Date of Birth: &

Training required: &

Current qualifications: &

Date of Application: &

Contact Adviser: &
```

Task 5

Retrieve the file **TASK4** if it is not already on your screen, and complete the form with the appropriate information from the message below. Save and print your work – use the filename **TASK5**.

Memo

From: Tina Davidson, Assistant Manager
To: Evie Raynor, Bedford St Manager
Date: 2/9/93

I took a telephone call from a Miss Susan Whitham yesterday afternoon enquiring about a training programme in word processing & accounts. She lives at 27 Mount Crossforth, Newcastle Upon Tyne, NE7 2BR and her date of birth is 28/10/54. Can you ask Beth Jones to act as her Contact Adviser – she can telephone Susan at home on 576 332. Susan already has RSA word processing stage 1 and GCSEs in English and Maths.

or at work on 682361

Task 6

Key in the following standard paragraphs. Save each one under the filename shown. (Use the copy below as a print-out check.)

Filename

AGENCY
```
TYNE TRAINING AGENCY
Woolford Road Centre
Woolford Road
NEWCASTLE UPON TYNE
NE6 5JL
```

ACCEPT
```
I am pleased to inform you that we are able to
accept you on to one of our training programmes.
```

APPOINT
```
The Centre will arrange an appointment for you to
see one of our training advisers for a comprehensive
guidance interview.
```

BROCHURE
```
Please find enclosed our latest brochure of training
programmes currently available. If there is
something not listed in the brochure, please do not
hesitate to bring this to our attention. We will do
everything we can to meet your personal needs.
```

YOURS
```
Yours sincerely
TYNE TRAINING AGENCY


Tina Davidson
ASSISTANT MANAGER
```

Task 7

Key in the letter below with a justified right margin. Recall the relevant paragraphs and insert at the points marked.

Save and print your work – use the filename **TASK7**.

AGENCY

Miss Susan Whitham

*see Task 5 for Susan Whitam's address

Dear Susan

Tyne Training Programmes ◄ CAPS + UNDERLINE

Following your recent telephone call, ACCEPT

✓   **In order to discuss your training needs and determine the type of ~~programme~~ training you require ~~I would like to arrange for you to see someone else~~ at our Bedford Street Centre and they will be contacting you ~~shortly.~~** asap APPOINT

have refd yr details to

BROCHURE

Also attached is a questionnaire for you to complete. ᐟ

Please
~~Please~~ **take this with you to the interview.** ◄

→ **Please don't hesitate to contact me again if you need any more help from me.**   Altho' you shd hear from yr adviser shortly

YOURS

We bel it will help us to dev the marketing ~~services~~ and publicity side of our org if we ~~are able to~~ collate info on client response to adverts etc.

Operator i(a) indent the paragraph beginning "Also attached is ———" by 12 spaces at left margin

b) standardise the paragraph styles throughout the letter to blocked style.

Task 8

Key in the table below. You may alter the line length or pitch if necessary to make it fit on an A4 page with the shorter end at the top.

Save and print your work – use the filename **TASK8**.

```
TYNE TRAINING AGENCY
Woolford Road Centre
Woolford Road
NEWCASTLE UPON TYNE
NE6 5JL
```

TRAINING PROGRAMMES ADDITIONAL

The following list of training programmes is ~~to be included and are~~ additional to those outlined in the current brochure. We are able to offer a 50% reduction in course fees for people who are registered as unemployed.

PROGRAMME TITLE	COST £	NO OF WEEKS	COURSE DAY	DETAILS* TIME	HOURS
Book-keeping Beginners	75.00	12	Mon	1430	2.5
" "	75.00	12	Tues	1430	2.5
~~" "~~	~~75.00~~	~~12~~	~~Wed~~	~~1430~~	~~2.5~~
Book-keeping Intermediate	85.00	15	Mon	2 pm	2.0
" "	85.00	15	Tues	1930	2.0
Book-keeping Advanced	£85 ~~95.00~~	15	Wed	1430	2.5
" "	£85 ~~95.00~~	15	Wed	7 pm	2.5
Basic Accounting	65.0p	10	Tues	1330	3.0
Advanced Accounting	95.0p	10	Friday	1330	2.0

* Flexible open and distance learning packages also available with up to 25 per cent fee reductions - ask for all the details.

operator : a) don't use dittos - type words out in full

b) retain abbreviations for the days of the week

Re-arrange the table items in day order starting with the beginning of the week

Print-out checks

Exercise 1A

CALDERGHYLL (REF CMB424)

This mid-terraced house is near the centre of the town and convenient for all amenities. Luxuriously furnished with antiques and equipped with every labour-saving device, this house offers the ideal place for a relaxing break. Accommodation is for 4 people in 2 twin-bedded rooms on the first floor. The ground floor comprises lounge, kitchen and dining room. The first floor bathroom has both bath and shower.

The owner does not object to one small dog kept under proper control.

PRICE BAND 12   NB Available from (correct date inserted for 1st Saturday of next month).

Exercise 1B

There is no reason why you should not buy overdue products because the shopkeeper is obliged to provide goods which meet a certain quality - they must not be "bad" or "off". Even if you buy such goods at a reduced price, your legal rights are not affected. If you are unable to obtain satisfaction from the shop manager, contact the local Trading Standards Officer through the Town Hall.

Most food producers need to maintain a good reputation and they will usually take any complaint very seriously indeed. It is often a good idea to write to the Managing Director of an organisation enclosing, if possible, a sample of the defective goods. You may have your costs refunded and sometimes a free gift or sample is sent to you as a token of goodwill.

T S Orwen   (correct date inserted for 1st Friday of next month)

Exercise 2A

Ref EWP/2A

Date of typing

URGENT

Mrs B S Kelly
236 Main Street
Weston
BARNSLEY
BY10 8JJ

Dear Mrs Kelly

CUMBRIAN COTTAGES

Thank you for your letter of (correct date inserted for last Monday) requesting information on self-catering cottages in Cumbria. I have pleasure in setting out below details of the accommodation at "Calderghyll" which is available for the dates which you mentioned.

A booking form is enclosed for your use and I hope that you will find that you are satisfied with "Calderghyll" from the details shown. At this time of year many people are making holiday arrangements and I would suggest that you telephone our bookings section on 061-763205 as soon as possible in order to make a provisional reservation. You can telephone at any time between 8.00 am and 7.00 pm from Monday to Friday and between 10.00 am and 5.00 pm from Saturday to Sunday.

CALDERGHYLL (REF CMB424)

This mid-terraced house is near the centre of the town and convenient for all amenities. Luxuriously furnished with antiques and equipped with every labour-saving device, this house offers the ideal place for a relaxing break. Accommodation is for 4 people in 2 twin-bedded rooms on the first floor. The ground floor comprises lounge, kitchen and dining room. The first floor bathroom has both bath and shower.

The owner does not object to one small dog kept under proper control.

PRICE BAND 12   NB Available from (correct date inserted for 1st Saturday of next month).

Exercise 2A (continued)

I would like to take this opportunity of assuring you of the high standards of service which you can expect from our organisation.

We pride ourselves on the careful and thorough processing of enquiries and bookings. All of our properties are regularly inspected and members of staff are available at any time to solve any problems which may arise.

We recommend that you take advantage of our inexpensive insurance cover. The cost is competitive at £4.50 per person per week, and £15.00 for a family (4 to 6 persons).

Please contact me if you would like any further information or advice. I look forward to hearing from you in the near future.

Yours sincerely
RURAL IDYLLS PLC

Elisabeth W Pendragon

Enc

Exercise 2B

Ref TSO/WP/B2

(Date of typing)

FOR THE ATTENTION OF MS W GOOD

The Consumer Guide
172-175 Byre Street
YORK
YO2 1JM

Dear Sirs

LETTERS PAGE

I recently received a request from your organisation for a contribution to your Consumer Information column, which I have pleasure in setting out below.

NOT AT ITS BEST?

There is no reason why you should not buy overdue products because the shopkeeper is obliged to provide goods which meet a certain quality – they must not be "bad" or "off". Even if you buy such goods at a reduced price, your legal rights are not affected. If you are unable to obtain satisfaction from the shop manager, contact the local Trading Standards Officer through the Town Hall.

Most food producers need to maintain a good reputation and they will usually take any complaint very seriously indeed. It is often a good idea to write to the Managing Director of an organisation enclosing, if possible, a sample of the defective goods. You may have your costs refunded and sometimes a free gift or sample is sent to you as a token of goodwill.

T S Orwen   **(correct date inserted for 1st Friday of next month)**

It is possible that you are already aware of the fact that it is not unknown for certain people to take advantage of a manufacturer's generosity by frequently returning 'faulty' products. Most manufacturers keep records of these transactions so it is not a practice which I would recommend and it involves more time and effort than it is worth.

Although there is considerable expense in postage, some people have almost made a part-time job out of this hobby! Do you think that an extra paragraph to this effect would be useful or relevant for your readers?

Please let me know your decision both on the submitted text and the additional information.

2

Exercise 3A

Name   Unit 3   Exercise 3A

RURAL IDYLLS

            C U M B R I A N   C O T T A G E S

Self-catering cottages in Cumbria

At this time of year many people are making holiday
arrangements. Telephone our reservations section on 061-
763205 as soon as possible in order to make a provisional
reservation.

You can telephone at any time between 0800 hrs and 1900 hrs
from Monday to Friday and between 0900 hrs and 1700 hrs from
Saturday to Sunday.

You can be assured of high standards of service from our
organisation. We pride ourselves on the thorough and careful
processing of enquiries and reservations. All of our
properties are regularly inspected and members of staff are
available at any time to solve any problems which may arise.

We recommend that you take advantage of our inexpensive
insurance cover. The cost is competitive at £4.50 per person
per week, and £15.00 for a family (4 – 6 persons).

        THE CALDERBROOK AREA HAS 2 HOUSES WHICH ARE
        AVAILABLE WITHIN THE DATES REQUIRED.

                                                        1

Exercise 2B (continued)

FOOD ADDITIVES

I hope to hear from you as soon as possible on my article on
food additives as you said you may be interested in this.

I enclose my business card so that you may telephone me. I am
in full-time employment so you can reach me between the hours
of 9.00 am and 5.00 pm at my business number. After 6.00 pm I
can be contacted at home.

Yours faithfully

T S Orwen (Mr)

Enc

                                                        2

Exercise 3A (continued)

Name   Unit 3   Exercise 3A

RURAL IDYLLS

Brockholes Cottage (Ref CMB546)

This attractive stone cottage has been renovated to a very high standard. It is particularly well-equipped, having an automatic washer, tumble drier, dishwasher and microwave oven.

Accommodation is for 3 or 4 persons in 2 bedrooms (1 twin, 1 double). There is a comfortable sitting room with a log fire and a separate kitchen/diner. The modern bathroom has a 3-piece suite and there is a separate shower room on the ground floor.

The property has the advantages of:

    oil-fired central heating
    electricity for cooking
    garage for one car
    private walled garden

The owner does not object to 1 small dog kept under proper control.

The Cottage is 1 mile from shops and pub, and many clients have already made reservations.

PRICE BAND 10   NB Available from (correct date inserted for 2nd Saturday of next month).

3

Exercise 3A (continued)

Name   Unit 3   Exercise 3A

RURAL IDYLLS

Calderghyll (Ref CMB424)

This mid-terraced house is near the centre of Calderbrook and convenient for all amenities. Luxuriously furnished with antiques and equipped with every labour-saving device, this house offers the ideal place for a relaxing break.

Accommodation is for 4 people in 2 twin-bedded rooms on the first floor. The ground floor comprises lounge, kitchen and dining room. The first floor bathroom has both bath and shower.

The owner does not object to 1 small dog kept under proper control.

PRICE BAND 12   NB Available from (correct date inserted for 1st Saturday of next month).

2

Exercise 3B

Name   Exercise 3B

Shoppers Guide

L E T T E R S   P A G E

NOT AT ITS BEST?

My local shop sometimes sells products at the end of their 'sell by' date at reduced prices. Is it safe to buy these?

There is no reason why you should not buy overdue products because the shopkeeper is obliged to provide products which meet a certain quality. Even if you buy such products at a reduced price, your legal rights are not affected. If you are unable to obtain satisfaction from the shop manager, contact the local Trading Standards Officer at the Town Hall.

Most food producers need to maintain their reputation and they take complaints very seriously indeed. It is often a good idea to write to the Managing Director of an organisation enclosing, if possible, a sample of the defective products. You may have your costs refunded and sometimes a free sample or gift is sent to you as a token of goodwill.

LETTERS   1

Exercise 3B (continued)

Name   Exercise 3B

Shoppers Guide

You may be aware of the fact that certain people take advantage of a manufacturer's generosity by frequently returning 'faulty' products. However, most manufacturers keep records of these transactions so it is not a practice which I would recommend and it involves a lot of effort and expense.

FOOD ADDITIVES

I want to buy good food for my children. Can I believe what the manufacturers put on their labels?

The 1984 Food Labelling Regulations allowed the public to see exactly what they were eating although some of the names and numbers did not have much meaning.

As a result of pressure from certain organisations, many of the unnecessary chemicals have been removed from pre-packed foods and manufacturers now actively promote the 'wholesome' nature of their products.

LETTERS   2

Exercise 3B (continued)

Name   Exercise 3B

Shoppers Guide

However, as consumers we need to be wary of being fooled by claims such as:

    no added colour
    no additives
    no artificial ingredients
    no preservatives

Such claims may be true for a product but this does not mean that the food is nutritious. Always read the ingredient list.

PURE AND SIMPLE?

Some of the descriptions on food labels sound vague, eg 'flavour', 'pure', 'natural'. What do they really mean?

Flavour is a misleading description – a 'raspberry flavour'

food need not contain any raspberry at all! A 'raspberry

flavoured' food should obtain a large part of its flavour from

raspberries, whereas a 'raspberry' food must be made with

whole raspberries. Secret ingredients can creep into some

products. Small amounts of sugar and preservatives do not

have to be declared so it is difficult to be sure whether

products are really 'pure' and 'natural'.

LETTERS   PAGE

LETTERS

Exercise 4A

Name   Exercise 4A

SYNOPSIS OF PRESENTATION

A wide range of everyday things can be turned into wine and the results are often very palatable and cheap to produce. Berries, flowers, vegetables, fruits, leaves and weeds can all be transformed into interesting and colourful drinks.

Many suitable ingredients can be found in your garden (or in someone else's) so it is not always necessary to visit the greengrocer. You don't need to spend a lot of money on equipment and there are many shops and supermarkets offering everything you will need. However, you must always take great care in hygiene just as you would if you were preparing food.

Available Wednesdays from (correct date inserted for 2nd Wednesday of next month)

3

Exercise 4B

Name   Exercise 4B

Ref PC/WP/EX4B

(Date of typing)

FOR THE ATTENTION OF THE SPEAKER'S SECRETARY

Greenbank Centre
Greenbank Lane
DERBY
DE6 7JL

Dear Sirs

WINE-MAKING

I was pleased to receive your request for a presentation on
the above topic which I think would be of interest to members
of your organisation. A synopsis is given below.

SYNOPSIS OF PRESENTATION

A wide range of everyday things can be turned into wine and
the results are often very palatable and cheap to produce.
Berries, flowers, vegetables, fruits, leaves and weeds can all
be transformed into interesting and colourful drinks.

Many suitable ingredients can be found in your garden (or in
someone else's) so it is not always necessary to visit the
greengrocer. You don't need to spend a lot of money on
equipment and there are many shops and supermarkets offering
everything you will need. However, you must always take great
care in hygiene just as you would if you were preparing food.

Available Wednesdays from (correct date inserted for 2nd
Wednesday of next month)

I would be obliged if you could let me know the date you would
prefer as soon as possible as I have other organisations
regularly contacting me, and I need a certain amount of time
to make sure that I have a sufficiently wide range of wines to
bring along to a demonstration.

A special feature of my talk is the opportunity to taste the
different wines as well as being able to take away a copy of
the easiest recipes. I will supply the wine if you will
supply the glasses! I enclose one copy of my Recipes sheet
which you are welcome to photocopy as necessary.

Exercise 4B (continued)

Name   Exercise 4B

My talk usually lasts for about one hour, followed by
approximately half an hour for tasting and questions. I could
be at your Centre at 1830 hours. If the talk began at
1900 hours, I would anticipate leaving at approximately 2100
hours. I do not charge a fee but would be obliged if you
could let me have the token sum of £5 to cover expenses.

There are some items of wine-making equipment which I would
like to show you, and I would need a large table to
accommodate these.

Perhaps you could let me have directions and a map if possible
to help me to find the Greenbank Centre. It would also be of
great assistance to me if you could let me know where I can
park my car when I arrive. There is quite a lot of carrying
to be done both before and after the presentation so the
nearer I can get to the Centre, the better.

I look forward to hearing from you.

Yours faithfully

PENNY CROFTON (MRS)

Enc

2

Exercise 4C

Name　Exercise 4C

WINES FROM YOUR GARDEN

C O U N T R Y　W I N E - M A K I N G

A wide range of everyday things can be turned into wine and the results are often very palatable and cheap to produce. Berries, flowers, vegetables, fruits, weeds and leaves can all be transformed into interesting and colourful drinks.

Many suitable ingredients can be found in your garden (or in someone else's) so it is not always necessary to visit the greengrocer. You don't need to spend a lot of money on equipment and there are many shops and supermarkets offering everything you will need.

1

Exercise 4C (continued)

Name　Exercise 4C

WINES FROM YOUR GARDEN

BASIC FACTS

During my talk you had the opportunity to taste the different wines. My Recipes sheet gives some easy recipes.

The main stages of country wine-making are:

1　Extraction of flavour and colour

2　Addition of other ingredients and fermenting

3　Straining

4　Fermenting

5　Racking

6　Bottling

7　Storing – for at least six months

The main ingredient is the fruit, vegetables, flowers or herbs which give the wine its individual colour, taste and smell.

Yeast is the most important ingredient in country wine-making – it must be wine yeast – and a yeast nutrient should be added.

Sugar must be carefully weighed before it is made into a syrup, ie dissolved in hot water, and added to the 'must'.

2

Unit 5 Task 1

RETURNING TO WORK

One of the main concerns facing anyone who is considering returning to work after a few years is the inability to cope with new technology. This could affect people in any industry but the revolution in information technology has perhaps been the greatest change over a short period of time. A good retraining scheme offering hands-on experience with up-to-date equipment can help to allay some fears and, at the same time, provide the trainees with recognised qualifications in their chosen vocational area.

Women who have spent some time caring for a family may lack confidence and assume that they will have to return to routine work. It is important that these women become able to identify the skills they have acquired so that, with adequate training and encouragement, they can achieve their full potential and take their place in the world of work.

Exercise 4C (continued)

Name Exercise 4C

WINES FROM YOUR GARDEN

WINE-MAKING EQUIPMENT

It is not necessary to spend a lot of money on special equipment. You probably have most things in your kitchen already. However, you must always take great care in hygiene just as you would if you were preparing food.

Many supermarkets have a range of country wine-making equipment and there are specialist shops for the enthusiast.

Perhaps one of the most helpful aids is your cellar book where you can record details of each wine. You can have great fun, if you have artistic leanings, in designing your own labels.

Any kind of bottle will do for your wine provided it is a <u>wine</u> bottle. Restaurants are usually happy to give away their empties. You will also need:

corks
bottle brush
siphon hose
corking tool
straining cloths

A wide range of everyday things can be turned into wine and

the results are often very palatable and cheap to produce.

Unit 5 Task 2

Name   Task 2

Ref TSD/TRG-WR

(Date of typing)

FOR THE ATTENTION OF THE PERSONNEL OFFICER

Personnel and Training Department
North East Communications Group
Shield House
Shield Road
NEWCASTLE UPON TYNE
NE6 7YT

Dear Sirs

RECRUITMENT OF QUALIFIED OFFICE STAFF

I am writing to you as one of the major employers in the area to give you details about the service which my company can provide. We were established 5 years ago and have steadily grown so that we now employ 6 advisers at our agency in the city centre with 3 advisers at our Durham branch. Our special field is the placing of clerical and secretarial staff into both temporary and permanent positions and we take considerable care to match our clients with workers of the standard requested.

Before accepting a potential employee on to our 'books', we assess them to ensure that they have the necessary aptitude and ability. Educational certificates are checked and the level of current skills is tested on a typewriter or word processor.

Many of the people who come to our agency have not worked for some time and we offer them the opportunity to retrain with our parent company, Tyne Training.

One of the main concerns facing anyone who is considering returning to work after a few years is the inability to cope with new technology. This could affect people in any industry but the revolution in information technology has perhaps been the greatest change over a short period of time. A good retraining scheme offering hands-on experience with up-to-date equipment can help to allay some fears and, at the same time, provide the trainees with recognised qualifications in their chosen vocational area.

Women who have spent some time caring for a family may lack confidence and assume that they will have to return to routine work. It is important that these women become able to identify the skills they have acquired so that, with adequate training and encouragement, they can achieve their full potential and take their place in the world of work.

Unit 5 Task 2 (continued)

Name   Task 2

Tyne Training is able to offer such women the training they need. Programmes are designed to suit individual needs after an initial assessment by qualified advisers. The trainees can brush up on their previous knowledge and skills and have the latest electronic office equipment at their disposal. Women who have not worked in an office environment before take a full programme starting with keyboard skills. Assessment is practical in nature and trainees are reviewed regularly.

An Information Day is to be held at Tyne Training's Woolford Road Centre on Friday of next week, between 1.00 pm and 7.00 pm. An invitation and full details are enclosed. Please let me know if you will be able to attend and the number of representatives which will be coming from your company. I look forward to meeting you.

Yours sincerely
TYNE EMPLOYMENT AGENCY

Tina Davidson
ASSISTANT MANAGER

Encs

2

Unit 5 Task 3

Name Task 3   TYNE TRAINING

TYNE EMPLOYMENT AGENCY
AND
TYNE TRAINING

I N F O R M A T I O N   D A Y

Friday (date inserted) from 1.00 pm to 7.00 pm

Woolford Road Centre, Woolford Road, NE6 5JL

TRAINING TOMORROW'S OFFICE STAFF TODAY

TYNE EMPLOYMENT AGENCY

We were established 5 years ago and have steadily grown so that we now employ 6 advisers at our agency in the city centre with 3 advisers at our Durham branch. Our special field is the placing of clerical and secretarial staff into both temporary and permanent positions and we take considerable care to provide our clients with workers of the standard requested.

Before accepting a potential employee, we assess them to ensure that they have the necessary aptitude and ability. Educational certificates are checked and the level of current skills is tested on a typewriter or word processor.

TYNE TRAINING

Many of the people who come to our agency have not worked for some time and we offer them the opportunity to retrain with our parent company, Tyne Training.

One of the main concerns facing anyone who is considering returning to work after a few years is the inability to cope with new office technology. A good retraining scheme offering hands-on experience with up-to-date equipment can help to allay some fears and, at the same time, provide the students with recognised qualifications in their chosen vocational area.

It is important that women returners become able to identify the skills they have so that, with adequate training and encouragement, they can achieve their full potential and take their place in the world of work.

1

Unit 5 Task 3 (continued)

Name Task 3   TYNE TRAINING

Tyne Training is able to offer such women the training they need. Programmes are designed to suit individual needs after an initial assessment by qualified advisers. The students can brush up on their previous knowledge and skills and have the latest electronic office equipment at their disposal. Women who have not worked in an office environment before take a full programme starting with keyboard skills. Assessment is practical in nature and each student's progress is reviewed regularly.

Our training programmes are designed to accommodate individual needs. The 'core' curriculum covers:

1   Text processing skills
2   Administrative procedures
3   Electronic office

Options may be added from the following list after initial assessment:

Shorthand

Audio-typewriting

French for the Office

When we are satisfied that a student has reached a good level of ability, we assist him or her to find work. Specialist tutors guide students through the process of looking for a suitable position, applying for the post, preparing for an interview, and finally getting through the actual interview successfully.

TRAINING TOMORROW'S OFFICE STAFF TODAY

2

Unit 5 Task 3 (continued)

Name Task 3   TYNE TRAINING

TYNE EMPLOYMENT AGENCY
AND
TYNE TRAINING

I N F O R M A T I O N   D A Y

Friday (date inserted) from 1.00 pm to 7.00 pm

Woolford Road Centre, Woolford Road, NE6 5JL

LOOKING FOR THE BEST STAFF?

Tyne Training's Woolford Road Centre will be open to visitors
from commerce and industry. If you are interested in
recruiting first-class personnel, call in and see our students
at work. You'll be impressed by their efficiency and the wide
range of skills they have at their fingertips!

LOOKING FOR THE BEST TRAINING?

The Tyne Training Centre can help you. Ask about our wide
range of 'personalised' programmes, free training and
excellent results. See the students in action. Ask them
about the Centre – they are our best advocates!

SPECIALIST STAFF WILL BE AVAILABLE TO DEAL WITH YOUR QUERIES
ON RECRUITMENT OR TRAINING.

Refreshments provided

TRAINING TOMORROW'S OFFICE STAFF TODAY

3

Exercise 6C

BRITANNIA BULBS ORDER FORM
26 Rocks Road
Sheffield
S4 7JB

Customer Name: Mrs J Smithies   Tel No: 0274 384572

Address: Woodnook Cottage
Woodnook Close
BRADFORD

Post Code: BD5 TR2

Bulbs Type: Tulips

Variety: Queen Alicia

Cat No: TU3782

Quantity: 3 dozen

Price: £2.35 per dozen

Date of Order: 15 July 1992

Method of Payment: Cheque

TO BE COMPLETED BY DESPATCH DEPARTMENT

Despatch Date .... Despatched by ....

Exercise 6D

```
                    BRITANNIA BULBS ORDER FORM
                         26 Rocks Road
                           Sheffield
                            S4 7JB

Customer Name: Walter Riley

Address: 4 Bridge Lane
         HUDDERSFIELD

Post Code: HD2 FL8              Tel No: 0484 37625

Bulbs Type: Crocus

Variety: Mixed

Cat No: CR2212

Quantity: 5 dozen

Price: £1.50 per dozen

Date of Order: 16 July 1992

Method of Payment: Visa
--------------------------------------------------------
TO BE COMPLETED BY DESPATCH DEPARTMENT

Despatch Date .......... Despatched by ..............
```

Exercise 6E

```
W H BRIDGES & CO                              Branch No: 346
SALES PROMOTION - WEEKEND RESIDENTIAL

PERSONNEL ACCOMMODATION DETAILS

Branch: LEEDS

Branch Tel No: 0532 683462

No of Personnel attending: 2
Name(s) of Personnel: Chris Blanchard
                      Diane Whitely

Date of Residential: From: 2 August 1993    To: 3 August 1993

Accommodation required: 2 single rooms with bath

Attendance confirmed on (date): 27 July 1993
```

Exercise 7B

BRITANNIA BULBS
26 Rocks Road
Sheffield
S4 7JB

Tel No: 0742 472831

(today's date)

Mrs J Smithies
Woodnook Cottage
Woodnook Close
BRADFORD BD5 2TR

Dear Mrs Smithies

RE YOUR ORDER OF 15 JULY 1993

Thank you for your recent order for a selection of our bulbs.

Our records show your order was for: 3 dozen Tulips, Queen Alicia variety at a cost of £2.35 per dozen.

We are pleased to advise you that these items are in stock and should arrive within the next fourteen days.

A receipt for your cheque will be enclosed with the bulbs, along with instructions for planting.

We look forward to hearing from you again.

Yours sincerely
BRITTANIA BULBS

Sales Department

Exercise 7C

BRITANNIA BULBS
26 Rocks Road
Sheffield
S4 7JB

Tel No: 0742 472831

(today's date)

Mr Walter Riley
4 Bridge Lane
HUDDERSFIELD
HD2 8FL

Dear Mr Riley

Thank you for your recent order for a selection of our bulbs.

Our records show that your order was for 5 dozen Mixed Crocus bulbs, Cat No CR2212, and that you have already paid in full by VISA.

We are sorry to advise you that these items are currently out of stock. In fact, your order was taken from a catalogue which was out-of-date. Please find enclosed an up-to-date price list and this season's brochure.

We will be pleased to supply you with an alternative selection from the new catalogue or offer you a full refund. Please accept our apologies for any inconvenience caused, along with the attached 50p voucher.

Yours sincerely
BRITTANIA BULBS

Sales Department

Encs

Exercise 7D

BRITANNIA BULBS
26 Rocks Road
Sheffield
S4 7JB

Tel No: 0742 472831

(today's date)

H Jones & Son
Beaver Works
Drye Road
HALIFAX
HX4 8UY

Dear Sirs

Thank you for your recent enquiry regarding a selection of our bulbs.

We are pleased to hear of your intentions to improve the firm's car-parking area with bulbs and shrubbery, and would like to take this opportunity to tell you about our new Garden Helpline Service.

Details of this are explained in the accompanying leaflet, along with our new Gardener's Helpline Telephone Number.

When returning your order form, could you please let us know where you saw our advertisement as this will assist our marketing department.

Please find enclosed an up-to-date price list and this season's brochure.

Yours faithfully
BRITTANIA BULBS

Sales Department

Encs

Exercise 8B

BRITTANIA BULBS

LATEST ADDITIONS TO THE CATALOGUE:

BULB DESCRIPTION	CAT NO	PRICE	UNIT
SPRING FLOWERING			
CROCUS – Purple Delight . . .	CR2213	1.65	dozen
IRIS – Lilac Lady . . .	IRI21	2.40	dozen
TULIP – Princess Orange Maiden . . .	TU3784	3.50	dozen
ANENOME – Rainbow Palette . . .	AN8167	4.55	fifty
SPECIAL SPRING MIXTURE* . . .	SB14	10.00	hundred
AUTUMN FLOWERING			
ZEPHYRANTHES – Autumn Breeze . . .	ZE13	0.45	each
GLADIOLUS – White Heat . . .	GL36	0.75	three
ACIDANTHERA – Princess Rhia . . .	AC3334	0.95	each
SPECIAL AUTUMN MIXTURE . . .	SB14	15.00	hundred

* Also available in Units of 500 at a Discount Price of £35.00

Exercise 8C

W H BRIDGES & CO SALES PROMOTION

WEEKEND RESIDENTIAL

The following personnel are to be directly involved with the company's new sales promotion scheme. Their names need to be added to the attendance list for the weekend residentials to be held in August.

DETAILS OF BRANCHES NO	NAME	PAYROLL NO	NAME	DATE OF W/R*
311	BRADFORD	37268	ASHRAF AKBAR	10/8/92
237	YORK	27346	SUSANNAH BLAKELY	17/8/92
346	LEEDS	23672	CHRIS BLANCHARD	3/8/92
237	YORK	18384	CHRISTOPHER BLAND	17/8/92
119	HUDDERSFIELD	27474	MARTIN HOLROYD	24/8/92
119	HUDDERSFIELD	36272	STEPHAN ITRYCH	24/9/92
314	SHEFFIELD	37283	MAVIS RAWSON	10/8/92
311	BRADFORD	28473	MARGARET SUNCLIFFE	10/8/92
346	LEEDS	24671	DIANE WHITELY	3/8/92

* The Weekend Residentials start on the dates listed in the table above but a number of personnel will require an overnight stay the previous night – details of these to follow shortly.

Exercise 8D

MUSIC PROMOTIONS LTD

SPECIAL OFFERS

We are pleased to announce this month's special offers. All units are supplied in black ash effect finish. Special discounts are available on bulk orders (25 or more).

ITEM DESCRIPTION	SIZE	CAT NO	PRICE
DEXCEL 2-drawer compact disc storage unit	12x12x7 in	WR114	5.25
NEWSTYLE cassette carousel	7x7x10 in	ZX727	3.99
REGENT 3-drawer audio cassette storage cabinet	14x12x7 in	ZX235	14.99
STAVER 4-drawer compact disc library cabinet	13x5x16 in	WR256	12.99
XENON de-luxe audio cassette storage case*	7x7x11 in	ZX551	5.49

* This item also available in luxury, green leather-look vinyl.

Exercise 9B

THE THREE EAGLES HOTEL

WEDDING RECEPTION BOOKING FORM

NAME Susan Bailey
ADDRESS 2 Grandsmere Place, Manchester
TEL NO 061-4782001

NO OF GUESTS
150

ROOM REQUIRED
Atlantic

RECEPTION DATE
September 12

RECEPTION TIME
1.30 pm - 4.30 pm

TYPE OF CATERING REQUIRED
Carvery

COST OF CATERING (per head)
£7.50

COST OF ROOM
£55.00

DATE
18 July

DEPOSIT PAID
£50.00

Exercise 9D

THE THREE EAGLES HOTEL
4 Grandways Road
MANCHESTER   MN4 ET2

(today's date)

Miss Susan Bailey
2 Grandsmere Place
MANCHESTER

Dear Susan

WEDDING RECEPTION

I am pleased to confirm the provisional booking for your wedding reception to take place on 12 September.

CATERING

I believe you have requested CARVERY-style catering @ £7.50 per head. As an alternative, you may wish to consider our hot and cold Buffet menus. Please find enclosed some sample menus of all our catering options.

ROOM

You have been allocated the ATLANTIC ROOM which will comfortably hold between 125-160 guests and will therefore accommodate your present guest list.

A fixed charge of £55 is payable for the room. Should you find you need to cater for additional guests, we can offer a larger room at no extra cost providing you notify us within the next month.

ACCOMMODATION

I understand you have relatives attending the function who wish to book an overnight stay at the Hotel. Please send us details of any requirements as soon as possible.

I shall contact you again in due course to make final arrangements.

Best wishes

Jane Lumb (MANAGERESS)

Encs

Exercise 9E

```
                THE THREE EAGLES
                4 Grandways Road
                MANCHESTER  MN4 ET2

FUNCTION BOOKINGS - SEPTEMBER

Hotel rooms have been booked for the
following dates in September. Please
arrange for temporary staff to be
contracted for all events, but
particularly where there are high guest
numbers.

CLIENT NAME          MENU         COST (£)    GUEST   DATE
                                  PER HEAD    NOS     BOOKED

Margaret Helm        CARVERY       7.50       100     2 SEP
Mohammed Zafar       HOT BUFFET    6.50       125     8 SEP
Susan Bailey         CARVERY       7.50       155     12 SEP
Anabella Ferrybridge HOT BUFFET    6.50       60      13 SEP
Henry Swan           CHEESE/WINE   4.75*      50      18 SEP
David Ridgeway       COLD BUFFET   5.50       85      20 SEP
Sebastian MacIntosh  COLD BUFFET   5.50       100     22 SEP
Betty Walsden        CARVERY       7.50       145     26 SEP

* Cost per head conditional on available house wines.
```

Unit 10 Task 5

```
TYNE EMPLOYMENT AGENCY
NEWCASTLE UPON TYNE

APPLICANT DETAILS

Name: SUSAN WHITHAM

Address: 27 MOUNT CROSSFORTH
         NEWCASTLE UPON TYNE
         NE7 2BR

Tel No:  Home: 576332
         Work: 682361

Date of Birth: 28 OCTOBER 1954

Training required: WORD PROCESSING, ACCOUNTS

Current qualifications: RSA WORDPROCESSING STAGE I
                        GCSE ENGLISH
                        GCSE MATHEMATICS

Date of Application: 1 SEPTEMBER 1993

Contact Adviser: BETH JONES
```

Unit 10 Task 7

TYNE TRAINING AGENCY
Woolford Road Centre
Woolford Road
NEWCASTLE UPON TYNE
NE6 5JL

(today's date)

Miss Susan Whitham
22 Mount Crossforth
NEWCASTLE UPON TYNE
NE7 2BR

Dear Susan

TYNE TRAINING PROGRAMMES

Following your recent telephone call, I am pleased to inform you that we are able to accept you on to one of our training programmes.

In order to discuss your training needs and determine the type of training programme you require I have referred your details to our Bedford Street Centre and they will be contacting you as soon as possible. The Centre will arrange an appointment for you to see one of our training advisers for a comprehensive guidance interview.

Please find enclosed our latest brochure of training programmes currently available. If there is something not listed in the brochure, please do not hesitate to bring this to our attention. We will do everything we can to meet your personal needs.

Also attached is a questionnaire for you to complete. Please take this with you to the interview. We believe it will help us to develop the marketing and publicity side of our organisation if we collate information on client response to advertisements etc.

Although you should hear from your adviser shortly, please don't hesitate to contact me again if you need any more help from me.

Yours sincerely
TYNE TRAINING AGENCY

Tina Davidson
ASSISTANT MANAGER

Encs

Unit 10 Task 8

TYNE TRAINING AGENCY
Woolford Road Centre
Woolford Road
NEWCASTLE UPON TYNE
NE6 5JL

ADDITIONAL TRAINING PROGRAMMES

The following list of training programmes are additional to those outlined in the current brochure. We are able to offer a 50% reduction in course fees for people who are registered as unemployed.

PROGRAMME TITLE	COST £	NO OF WEEKS	COURSE DETAILS* DAY	TIME	HOURS
Book-keeping Beginners	75.00	12	Mon	1430	2.5
Book-keeping Intermediate	85.00	15	Mon	1400	2.0
Book-keeping Beginners	75.00	12	Tues	1430	2.5
Book-keeping Intermediate	85.00	15	Tues	1930	2.0
Basic Accounting	65.00	10	Tues	1330	2.0
Book-keeping Advanced	85.00	15	Wed	1430	2.5
Book-keeping Advanced	85.00	15	Wed	1900	2.5
Advanced Accounting	95.00	10	Fri	1330	3.0

* Flexible distance and open learning packages also available with up to 25% fee reductions – ask for details.

Progress review checklist

Unit no.	Topic	Date completed	No. of errors
1	Proofreading skills		
	Print a document from the file directory		
	Change the line length of a document		
	Key in accurately from manuscript copy		
	Identify and correct typographical errors		
2	Identify inconsistencies in presentation of text		
	Key in text with consistency of presentation		
	Insert headers and footers on a document		
	Insert page numbering on a letter		
	Insert page breaks in a two-page letter		
	Expand recognized RSA II abbreviations		
	Identify text correction signs and amend text accordingly		
3	Insert page breaks in a multi-page document		
	Format text to a specified layout		
	Work logically through the editing of a document		
	Move around the document using quick methods		
	Delete text using 'quick' methods		
	Search and replace text globally		
	Align text to the right		
	Use headers, footers and page numbering effectively		
	Print documents from the file directory		
4	Complete consolidation 1 exercises as revision of theory and practice		
5	Complete mock examination paper for RSA Stage II Part 1		
6	Use search facility to locate entry points on a standard form		
	Complete a form with given information		
7	Set up standard paragraphs		
	Retrieve standard paragraphs into a document as instructed		
	Produce standard business letters using a standardized layout		
8	Work out tab settings for an advanced table display		
	Adapt a table to fit on the specified paper size		
	Rearrange table items in a specified order		
	Enter subdivided and/or multi-line column headings		
	Change the pitch size of the table text/numbers		
	Enter footnotes on to a table		
9	Complete consolidation 2 exercises as revision of theory and practice		
10	Complete mock examination paper for RSA Stage II Part 2		